LOUS
FEARLESS
MAESTRO
NEE
W9-DAB-527
GIRLS
ACCOMPLISHED
TENACIOUS
SUPER
T
ACE
SUPER
SAVVY
FEISTY
INSTINCTIVE
EXTRAORDINARY
ARTISTIC
GIRLS
CREATIVE
INCLUS
SUPER
CONQUERING
SOCIALLY-FOCUSED

THIS BOOK
BELONGS TO A
SUPERGIRL NAMED

MIGHTY

IS
PASSIO
MAESTRO
OUTSPOKEN
DEFIANT
RECORD-BREAKING
SUPER
MARVELL
GIRLS
EXPERT
BRAVE
POWERFUL
SUPER
REVOLUTIO
RLS
FEISTY
ILLUSTRIOUS
GIRLS
ACCOM

STORIES FOR SOUTH ASIAN SUPER GIRLS

PUFFIN BOOKS

UK | USA | Canada | Ireland | Australia
India | New Zealand | South Africa

Puffin Books is part of the Penguin Random House group of companies
whose addresses can be found at global.penguinrandomhouse.com.

www.penguin.co.uk   www.puffin.co.uk   www.ladybird.co.uk

Penguin
Random House
UK

First published in Great Britain by Kashi House CIC 2019
This edition published by Puffin Books 2021

001

Copyright © Raj Kaur Khaira, 2019, 2021
Illustrations by Anu Chouhan, Deepikah R. Bhardwaj, Kokila Bhattacharya, Meenal Patel,
Nazrina Rodjan, Poonam Saini, Rajvinder Kaur, Sandeep Johal, Suman Kaur and Vinny Soor

The moral right of the author and illustrators has been asserted

Printed in Italy

The authorized representative in the EEA is Penguin Random House Ireland,
Morrison Chambers, 32 Nassau Street, Dublin D02 YH68

A CIP catalogue record for this book is available from the British Library

ISBN: 978–0–241–55435–7

All correspondence to:
Puffin Books, Penguin Random House Children's
One Embassy Gardens, 8 Viaduct Gardens, London SW11 7BW

The publisher does not have any control over and does not assume any
responsibility for author or third-party websites or their content

STORIES FOR SOUTH ASIAN SUPER GIRLS

BY RAJ KAUR KHAIRA

PUFFIN

THIS IS FOR
THE SUPERGIRLS OUT
THERE ABOUT TO MAKE
THEIR MARK

★

CONTENTS

INTRODUCTION XI

 NOOR JAHAN 2

 ANJALI SUD 4

 DEEYAH KHAN 6

 CORNELIA SORABJI 8

 FARRAH STORR 10

 MONICA ALI 12

 ROBINA MUQIMYAR 14

 LHAKPA SHERPA 16

 BANNU PAN DEI 18

 M.I.A. 20

 RUCHI SANGHVI 22

★ NADIYA HUSSAIN 24

 SANA JAVERI KADRI 26

HANNAH SIMONE 28

 JHUMPA LAHIRI 30

NOOR INAYAT KHAN 32

 REETA LOI 34

★ JAMEELA JAMIL 36

 KALPANA CHAWLA 38

SANIA MIRZA 40

 AANCHAL MALHOTRA 42 ★

 ARUNDHATI ROY 44

★ PRITAM KAUR HAYRE 46

LILLY SINGH 48

 ANOUSHKA SHANKAR 50

SHABANA AZMI 52

 MAHARANI JIND KAUR 54

 MEERA SYAL 56

★ NEELAM GILL 58

AMRITA SHER-GIL 60

MIRA NAIR 62

 RUPI KAUR 64

 SOPHIA DULEEP SINGH 66

KARPAL KAUR SANDHU 68

 SHARMEEN OBAID-CHINOY 70

TIA KANSARA 72

 JHANSI KI RANI 74

MINDY KALING 76

 RAVINDER BHOGAL 78

IMTIAZ DHARKER 80

 JAYABEN DESAI 82

SHAINA AZAD 84

 NORAH JONES 86

RAZIA SULTAN 88

GAZAL DHALIWAL 90

INDRA NOOYI 92

SANA AMANAT 94

BEGUM SAMRU 96

RACHEL ROY 98

SUNAINA SETHI 100

YOUR STORY 102

YOUR PORTRAIT 103

TIMELINE 104

THE SUPER ARTISTS 109

ACKNOWLEDGEMENTS 130

ABOUT THE AUTHOR 131

INTRODUCTION

DEAR READER,

I remember the first time I read about Pritam Kaur Hayre. I was casually scrolling through Facebook when I came across an article about her.

I was amazed by how this uneducated woman from India (who also looked so much like my grandma) was virtually unknown despite accomplishing so much. Her story moved me so deeply, I found myself telling it to every South Asian woman I knew. It happened again when I learned about Kalpana Chawla. Then again with Razia Sultan.

I felt sad that I was so shocked to learn about the incredible achievements of these women. It was a sign of how little I knew about my own heritage and how the mainstream media rarely covered inspiring stories of South Asian women.

This bothered me for months and eventually I vowed to get these women's stories into everyone's hands. This book is my way of fulfilling that promise.

I aspire to live in a world where stories about South Asian women and their intelligence, bravery and talent aren't surprising but commonplace, where every brown girl grows up feeling worthy, inspired and capable.

When you look through these pages I hope you are able to see the amazing legion of women you have descended from and can call your own. I hope their stories echo in your soul as loudly as they did in mine. I hope their legacies inspire you to live the life of your dreams.

LOVE, RAJ

THE SUPER WOMEN

NOOR JAHAN

MIGHTY EMPRESS

'LIGHT OF THE WORLD.'

When Noor Jahan struck coins in her own name, it was a bold statement. She is the only Mughal empress to have done so. She deserved it because hers was the real power behind one of the world's most powerful and wealthy empires.

Born Mehr-un-Nissa, her family moved from Afghanistan to India to seek a better life when she was a baby. As her father rose up the ranks in the Mughal Empire, his fiercely intelligent daughter benefited from the best education available – languages, art, literature, dance and music would become her lifelong passions.

One day in 1611, Emperor Jahangir caught a glimpse of Mehr and immediately fell in love. They quickly married and became inseparable as a couple. When they went hunting together, Mehr excelled at shooting ferocious tigers. To honour his wife's strength, intellect and friendship, Jahangir began to call her by a new name: Noor Jahan or 'Light of the World'.

When Jahangir became ill, he asked Noor to step into his role. Her power grew steadily and Noor began to receive dignitaries, make political decisions and introduce important social and cultural changes. It became abundantly clear that even though Jahangir was emperor, Noor was the one in charge.

When rebels imprisoned her husband, she came to his rescue. Showing immense courage, Noor led her army into battle atop a war elephant. Though captured, she planned a daring escape and freed both herself and her husband.

Jahangir's death in 1627 led to chaos that damaged the Mughal Empire. Although Noor lost her power to a new emperor, this intelligent and capable ruler left a legacy that shines as brightly as her name.

BORN: 31 MAY 1577   DIED: 17 DECEMBER 1645 (AGED 68)
COUNTRY OF BIRTH: PRESENT-DAY AFGHANISTAN

ILLUSTRATION BY
MEENAL PATEL

ANJALI SUD

TENACIOUS BUSINESSWOMAN

'LIVE OUTSIDE YOUR COMFORT ZONE.'

This was the advice Anjali received from her father when she was young and they are the words she has lived by ever since.

Anjali grew up in the impoverished town of Flint, Michigan. Eager to get the best education available, the thirteen-year-old Anjali took her first bold leap and applied to a prestigious boarding school. She was accepted and was no longer afraid of taking risks. Anjali challenged herself again years later by attending Harvard, one of the best universities in the world.

Anjali went on to find work as a banker but wasn't passionate about her job. She realized she wanted to run companies but lacked experience.

So Anjali took a chance and accepted a summer internship at Amazon, one of the largest companies in the world.

Amazon were impressed by her work ethic and offered her a job in sales. Instead of accepting the offer, Anjali bravely asked to work in an area where she could make bigger decisions. Her courage paid off – Amazon listened and let her join their marketing team.

Before long, her father's advice was ringing in her ears and she knew she had to keep challenging herself. She left Amazon to join Vimeo, one of YouTube's biggest competitors. A combination of vision, talent and ambition propelled Anjali to the top of the company and she became Vimeo's chief executive officer at the age of just thirty-four!

Anjali's journey shows that the path to success is not simply a straight line – along the way there will be twists and turns, and highs and lows. For Anjali, failure and taking risks are essential to her success.

BORN: AUGUST 1983

COUNTRY OF BIRTH: UNITED STATES OF AMERICA

ILLUSTRATION BY
NAZRINA RODJAN

DEEYAH KHAN

POWERFUL FILMMAKER

'THE PRICE OF SILENCE IS FAR GREATER THAN TAKING A STAND.'

Despite receiving hate mail and death threats because of her work, Deeyah refuses to be silenced.

Deeyah was born in Oslo to a Pakistani father and an Afghan mother. Her father believed sports or music were the only two professions that didn't discriminate based on gender or race, so Deeyah chose to pursue music. She was a talented singer, giving her first television performance at the age of seven and releasing her first solo album when she was fifteen. Her career was controversial – some people from her community considered singing to be shameful and began to threaten her. Fearing for her safety, Deeyah left Norway for London. Sadly, the harassment continued and she had no choice but to abandon her music career.

Deeyah was devastated and spent the next two years considering what to do.

She was inspired by her South Asian fans, who continued to reach out to her even though she had retired from singing. Their messages weren't just fan mail – her fans shared their struggles, and asked Deeyah for help.

Deeyah felt compelled to educate the world about problems plaguing the South Asian community. She wanted to share stories in a meaningful way, so she picked up a camera and started to film. Her first film was a documentary about a young woman who had been tragically killed by her own family.

Deeyah's films are now used as part of police training programmes around the world. She has made six documentaries to date and has a catalogue of awards and nominations under her belt. Focusing on controversial subjects, Deeyah is on a quest to make the world a better place.

BORN: 7 AUGUST 1977
COUNTRY OF BIRTH: NORWAY

CORNELIA SORABJI

TRAILBLAZING LAWYER

'STUDY LAW WHEN THE TIME COMES.'

This advice was given to Cornelia by her mother after they heard how an elderly lady had been conned out of her land by her grandson. If Cornelia really wanted to help women, she would have to become a lawyer.

Cornelia was one of nine children raised in Pune. Her father, a community leader, recognized her intelligence at a young age and used his influence to convince Bombay University to allow women to study on their degree programmes. His campaigning paid off – Cornelia became its first woman graduate.

After graduating, Cornelia was denied a scholarship to study law in the UK despite meeting the requirements. Ever determined, she wrote letters to well-connected organizations requesting help. The response was overwhelming. Many English dignitaries, including Florence Nightingale, petitioned for her to be allowed to attend Oxford, one of the world's most famous universities.

Accepted in 1890, Cornelia made history by becoming the first woman to study law at Oxford. Back in India, however, she found most law firms were unwilling to hire a female lawyer. Cornelia began working for the maharajas but the cases were often trivial and bizarre – she was once forced to defend an elephant against its owner, the maharaja, who was also the judge!

Unable to practise law openly, Cornelia campaigned to become a legal adviser for vulnerable women. She is thought to have helped over 600 women and orphans fight their cases throughout her career.

Cornelia defied social norms and challenged discrimination in order to fight for women's rights in a system that tried its hardest to subdue her.

BORN: 15 NOVEMBER 1866   DIED: 6 JULY 1954 (AGED 87)
COUNTRY OF BIRTH: PRESENT-DAY INDIA

ILLUSTRATION BY
KOKILA BHATTACHARYA

FREEDOM

RIGHTS

FARRAH STORR

DYNAMIC EDITOR

'LIFE IS TOUGH BUT YOU ARE ULTIMATELY TOUGHER.'

When Farrah walked into her office, she was told yet another employee had quit her team. She had been the UK editor-in-chief of *Cosmopolitan* for only three months and eighty per cent of her staff had resigned. Farrah needed to find a way to restore the struggling magazine to its former glory.

Farrah grew up with a passion for journalism but her Pakistani father and English mother wanted her to become a doctor, engineer or lawyer. Luckily, Farrah's older sister paved the way when she changed her career, leaving her job as a lawyer to become a magazine writer.

While at university, Farrah did work experience at various magazines. The work was often unglamorous but she persisted and kept applying for writing jobs. After three long years of trying and more than fifty rejections, Farrah landed her first job in journalism. She built a strong reputation in the industry and, at the age of just thirty-three, she was hired to lead the UK launch of *Women's Health* magazine. Farrah's creative leadership helped it become a roaring success.

Farrah had long dreamed of working for *Cosmopolitan*, but they had always rejected her. Then, following her success at *Women's Health*, they asked Farrah to help them change the magazine's fortunes. Farrah made it look bolder, slicker and sharper, and introduced new topics, some of which attracted controversy. These changes upset most of the staff but sales rocketed. In only six months, *Cosmopolitan* was a best-seller again!

Farrah has won a number of awards for her editorial work and was named as one of the most powerful people in the UK. She has shown that, through sheer perseverance, it's possible to overcome huge obstacles.

BORN: 8 NOVEMBER 1978
COUNTRY OF BIRTH: UNITED KINGDOM

COSMOPOLITAN

AUTHOR

EDITOR

BODY POSITIVITY CHAMPION

MENTO

JOURNALIST

FEMINIST

ILLUSTRATION BY
RAJVINDER KAUR

MONICA ALI

MASTERFUL NOVELIST

'IF YOU THINK YOU ARE POWERLESS, THEN YOU ARE.'

This rousing line from Monica's debut novel summarizes her belief that women can succeed if they believe in themselves.

Born in Dhaka to an English mother and Bangladeshi father, Monica's family fled to the UK when she was four after civil war broke out in Bangladesh. But Monica's new life in the UK was not free from problems. Racism was on the rise and people were often attacked because of the colour of their skin. Despite this, Monica excelled at school and attended one of the world's best universities before starting a career in marketing.

After the birth of her first child, Monica became a home-maker. She joined an online short-story writing group for fun. Monica loved writing and realized that she needed to pen something more substantial to better express her ideas. After her second child was born, Monica began work on her first novel, *Brick Lane*, about a Bangladeshi woman who marries and moves to London.

Monica sent her first two chapters to a friend who worked in publishing, asking for feedback. Much to her surprise, she was offered a book deal a few days later! Balancing the demands of motherhood with her writing, she finished the book in just eighteen months.

Brick Lane was a sensation when it was released in 2003 – it won multiple awards, was translated into twenty-six languages and has sold over one million copies globally! It was even made into a film.

Monica's success proves what you can achieve if you believe in yourself.

BORN: 20 OCTOBER 1967
COUNTRY OF BIRTH: PRESENT-DAY BANGLADESH

ILLUSTRATION BY
POONAM SAINI

ROBINA MUQIMYAR

AMAZING ATHLETE

'STANDING ON THE TRACK FELT LIKE WINNING.'

When eighteen-year-old Robina stood, beaming, at the starting line for the 100-metre race in the Athens Olympics, she had already won. Just by being there, she was proof that Afghanistan was changing.

As a child, Robina never had the chance to run or try athletics. Afghanistan's strict rulers, the Taliban, didn't allow girls to play sports or go to school after the age of eight, and anyone caught breaking the law was savagely beaten. The Taliban lost power in 2001 and things started to change. When seventeen-year-old Robina heard that the Afghan Olympic organization was looking for athletes, she jumped at the chance to start running. Many Afghans were horrified – running just wasn't something that women did.

Ignoring her critics, Robina began to train. She ran barefoot in the national stadium, which had been badly damaged by the Taliban. At first, the cracked concrete track cut and bruised Robina's feet. She persevered and eventually found a pair of broken sandals to run in. Robina steadily improved her running times and was thrilled to be chosen as one of five athletes to represent Afghanistan in the 2004 Olympics. At the opening ceremony, Robina stood proudly as a representative of Afghan women. As fireworks exploded above the stadium, she was painfully reminded of her past and the bomb blasts she had lived through.

Although Robina didn't win her race, everyone in the Olympic stadium was delighted to see her compete. She ran in the Olympics again four years later. Robina served as a Member of Parliament in the Afghan government between 2019 and 2021. Robina entered politics in the hope of bringing about further change for the girls and women of Afghanistan.

BORN: 3 JULY 1986
COUNTRY OF BIRTH: AFGHANISTAN

ILLUSTRATION BY
DEEPIKAH R. BHARDWAJ

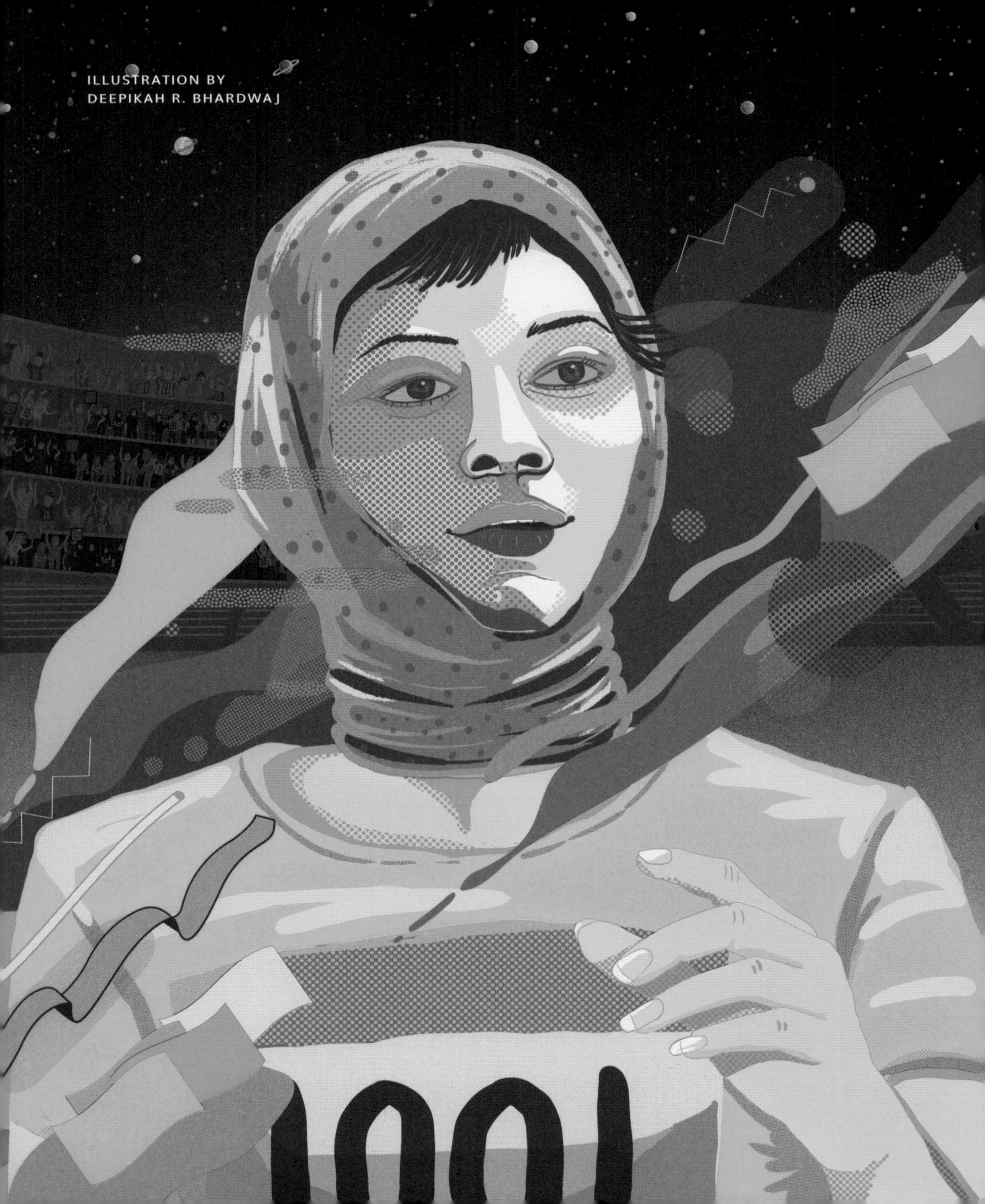

LHAKPA SHERPA

CONQUERING MOUNTAINEER

'I WANT TO PUSH MY LIMITS.'

On more than one occasion, Lhakpa has accomplished one of the toughest feats on the planet – climbing the highest mountain in the world, Mount Everest. She is so determined to conquer its peak that she has even climbed up it while two months pregnant!

Lhakpa was born in a small village in Nepal, 13,000 feet high in the Himalayan mountain range. Climbing came naturally to her and as a child she would often go on seven-hour hikes with her father.

When she was fifteen, Lhakpa began working for a mountaineering company. She spent her days hauling heavy equipment up and down dangerous slopes and quickly became an accomplished mountaineer.

Lhakpa dreamed of following in the footsteps of her idol, Pasang Lhamu. Pasang was the first Nepalese woman to scale Everest, but tragically perished on her way down.

Lhakpa finally got her chance to attempt her first ascent of Everest in 2000 as part of an all-woman team.

The towering mountain stands at 29,000 feet tall – that's the height at which planes fly! Fighting fierce winds, swirling snow and with a limited supply of oxygen, Lhakpa reached the rainbow-clad summit as dawn broke on 18 May 2000. After nearly two months of gruelling climbing, Lhakpa had finally accomplished her dream.

Since then, Lhakpa has braved frostbite, snow blindness, avalanches and earthquakes to conquer Everest eight more times. As of 2020, she was planning her tenth climb – more than any other woman in history.

BORN: 1973

COUNTRY OF BIRTH: NEPAL

ILLUSTRATION BY
MEENAL PATEL

BANNU PAN DEI

NOBLE IMMIGRANT

'THE GENERAL'S WIFE.'

These words, neatly written in gold letters on a headstone in a French coastal town's cemetery, describe a noblewoman named Bannu. She travelled thousands of miles with her beloved husband, settling in France at a time when very few Indian women lived in Europe.

Bannu was a charming and graceful girl who was raised in the mountains of northern India. She was chosen as a wife in her early youth by a French general, Jean François Allard. He had left Europe after the defeat of Napoleon and travelled to Punjab to serve Maharaja Ranjit Singh in 1822. Jean François was hired to train the army of the Sikh Empire.

Bannu and Jean François married in 1826, fell deeply in love and had several children. Jean François was allowed to settle his family in France.

They embarked on the long journey from Lahore to France, which took several months by sea, and reached Jean François's hometown of St Tropez in 1835. At first, Bannu was homesick but she gradually adjusted to her new life. However, her happiness was short-lived – just a year later Jean François had to return to Punjab to serve his king.

The couple wrote lovingly to one another even though letters took months to arrive. When Jean François died in 1839, Bannu was devastated and never accepted the news. She went to the port every evening, hoping to see his ship sailing in.

Bannu stayed in France for the rest of her life and eventually changed her religion to be closer to the spirit of her dear husband. Their story shows how love can be a bridge between cultures.

BORN: 25 JANUARY 1814   DIED: 13 JANUARY 1884 (AGED 69)
COUNTRY OF BIRTH: PRESENT-DAY INDIA

ILLUSTRATION BY
SANDEEP JOHAL

M.I.A.

FIERY SINGER

'MY MUSIC IS THE VOICE OF THE CIVILIAN REFUGEE.'

If Mathangi Arulpragasam had not left her war-torn country as a child refugee, she might not have become a renowned singer who uses her music to support oppressed people around the world.

Mathangi was just a baby when her family moved to Sri Lanka from London in 1975. When she was eight years old, a violent civil war erupted in Sri Lanka – even her school was bombed. Her family came back to London as refugees when Mathangi was ten. She overcame bullying and learning difficulties to complete a degree in fine art, film and video. In 2001, she returned to Sri Lanka to make a documentary about her childhood. The trip was a turning point for Mathangi – she witnessed widespread atrocities against Sri Lankan Tamils and resolved to do something about it.

Back in London, she adopted the name M.I.A. or 'Missing In Action' in remembrance of those who had disappeared without trace in the Sri Lankan civil war and began recording songs in various styles in her bedroom. As one of the first artists to share their music online, M.I.A. soon signed a record deal. She sang about refugees and conflict, freedom and oppression.

Since then, she has worked with many artists including Kanye West, Madonna and JAY-Z. While some have praised her, others have disagreed with M.I.A.'s messages and labelled her a terrorist. Her hard-hitting music videos were even banned from MTV and YouTube. This just made her more outspoken.

Describing herself as a bridge between East and West, M.I.A. was the first Asian to be nominated for Grammy and Oscar awards in the same year. M.I.A. is now known as the artist who draws on real-life experiences to give a voice to the voiceless.

BORN: 18 JULY 1975
COUNTRY OF BIRTH: UNITED KINGDOM

RUCHI SANGHVI

GROUNDBREAKING TECH GURU

'IT'S A MAN'S WORLD?'

When Ruchi told her dad she wanted to take over his machinery business, he told her it was a job for men. Dumbfounded by his dated view, she grew up determined to prove him wrong.

Born into a family of entrepreneurs in Pune, Ruchi dreamed of becoming a businesswoman. She soon moved to the US to study software engineering and was one of only five women in her class of 150 students.

After graduation, Ruchi worked in finance in New York. Within weeks, she knew it wasn't for her – she worked long hours and wasn't using any of her engineering knowledge. Before long, Ruchi quit and found work as a software engineer. Four months later, she saw a job advert – a new social media company called Facebook was looking for software engineers.

Ruchi applied and impressed the founder, Mark Zuckerberg, with her skills and enthusiasm during the interview. She joined the team of twenty employees and became Facebook's first female engineer. The work was hard and the hours long but Ruchi loved it.

One of Ruchi's first projects was Facebook's news feed. Launched in 2006, the feed allowed users to share information. But some people were outraged by the change. Despite criticism and even personal abuse, Ruchi kept working on the news feed. It is now one of Facebook's most successful features.

Ruchi worked at Facebook for nearly six years and saw the company grow to over 1,500 employees and one billion users.

Ruchi later set up her own successful businesses, proving that there's no job too big or difficult for a woman.

BORN: 20 JANUARY 1982
COUNTRY OF BIRTH: INDIA

ILLUSTRATION BY
POONAM SAINI

NADIYA HUSSAIN

BRAVE BAKER

'I'M NEVER GONNA SAY "I DON'T THINK I CAN" AGAIN. I CAN AND I WILL.'

As she stood in front of the cameras for the first time, Nadiya was nervous that the television audience would dismiss her as just another Muslim in a headscarf. However, simply by being herself, she would go on to win the country's adoration, proving she was just as British as anyone else.

Nadiya had a tough childhood growing up in Luton. She was bullied because of her dark skin and was often on the receiving end of hurtful racist remarks. Nadiya developed serious anxiety, but always found peace in the kitchen and so turned to baking to cope.

Nadiya was married with three children when she decided to start her university degree. Balancing everything was extremely demanding and, for the second time in her life, Nadiya turned to baking as a way to relax.

One day, her husband saw an advertisement asking bakers to enter *The Great British Bake Off*, the UK's most popular television cooking competition. He encouraged Nadiya to apply but it took her two years to summon the confidence to put herself forward. Much to her surprise, she was chosen to take part in the show.

The competition wasn't easy and Nadiya's anxiety and self-doubt nearly sabotaged her chances many times throughout the ten-week contest. Steadily though, her confidence grew. The judges were so impressed by her inventive bakes that they crowned her the winner in the show's finale in 2015.

Since winning, Nadiya has written books and hosted cooking shows on television.

Nadiya is living her dream and shattering stereotypes about women in headscarves along the way.

BORN: 25 DECEMBER 1984
COUNTRY OF BIRTH: UNITED KINGDOM

ILLUSTRATION BY
SUMAN KAUR

SANA JAVERI KADRI

ETHICAL ENTREPRENEUR

'NO ONE WAS DOING IT THE RIGHT WAY, SO MAYBE I SHOULD.'

When Sana first started selling high-quality turmeric to Americans, she was determined to improve the way people who were involved in the production of this nourishing Indian spice were treated.

Sana learned about eating healthily as a child in Mumbai. While her school friends were eating junk food, Sana's mother would give her brown bread and tofu. Later, Sana studied in California and, after graduating, began working in marketing at a grocery store. It was then that she realized just how popular turmeric was in America. However, despite being used for its health benefits, Sana realized that the spice being sold was often low in quality.

Sana also found out that the farmers who made it in India were being treated unfairly by big companies – while the farmers were paid about thirty-five cents

for a kilogram of turmeric, the companies would sell it for 100 times more! Sana resolved to stop this exploitation.

In 2017, Sana quit her job and went back to India. She spent half a year travelling across the country to source the freshest and highest-quality turmeric in the world. After agreeing to pay farmers ten times more than others did, she set up her company, Diaspora Co. Within two weeks of launching, she had secured approximately $10,000 worth of orders! Sana began selling more turmeric and the company quickly grew.

Sana ensures that everyone who works for her – from farmers to truck drivers – makes a living wage. She has proven that you can run a successful, profit-making business with a high-quality product and still treat your employees fairly.

BORN: 18 OCTOBER 1993
COUNTRY OF BIRTH: INDIA

HANNAH SIMONE

SOCIALLY FOCUSED ACTOR

'REPRESENTATION MATTERS.'

When Hannah burst onto the television scene in 2005, she was a breath of fresh air for Canada's ethnic minorities. Up until then, there had been hardly any South Asian faces on mainstream television.

Hannah grew up in a number of countries in Europe, the Middle East and Asia before moving to Canada to study at university.

Passionate about human rights from a young age, she decided to study how countries work together to solve problems. After graduating, Hannah was keen to change the world and went on to work at the United Nations, a global organization that encourages countries to cooperate. Hannah realized that many young people weren't getting involved in important social issues that would affect their future and she wanted to change that. To reach this underrepresented group, Hannah set her sights on becoming a television presenter who would educate the public.

Hannah landed her first television job as a VJ on Canada's largest music channel, MuchMusic. She used this platform to host the news and bring attention to climate change and AIDS. After a few years, Hannah moved to Hollywood to pursue a career in acting. She got a starring role in the hit television show *New Girl*, becoming one of the few South Asian women on American screens. Hannah has used her influence to support female representation in the film industry.

Hannah's timely appearance on screen has been a vital step in connecting young people to some of the world's most pressing problems and changing the types of acting roles given to ethnic minority actors.

BORN: 3 AUGUST 1980
COUNTRY OF BIRTH: UNITED KINGDOM

ILLUSTRATION BY
ANU CHOUHAN

JHUMPA LAHIRI

ACCOMPLISHED WORDSMITH

'I FELT NEITHER INDIAN NOR AMERICAN.'

Despite belonging to two cultures, Jhumpa always felt like she struggled to fit in. To combat her feelings of loneliness, she began to write.

Jhumpa moved from London to Rhode Island in the US at a young age, but always felt like an outsider. Her parents wanted her to be Bengali, but she spoke English, celebrated western holidays at school and had American friends. To help her cope with her dual identity, Jhumpa turned to books for comfort. Reading about amazing new worlds and incredible characters inspired Jhumpa to write her own stories.

Jhumpa continued to write while at university. She tried to get her short stories published but was rejected by several publishing companies. Her parents wanted her to get a secure job as a lecturer but Jhumpa decided to focus on developing her writing skills instead. In 1997, Jhumpa began writing *Interpreter of Maladies*, her first collection of short stories. The book explored loneliness and belonging – things that Jhumpa had experienced as a child.

This time Jhumpa managed to secure a publishing deal. Her book went on to win the coveted Pulitzer Prize for Fiction and has sold over 15 million copies worldwide!

Having lived in several countries, Jhumpa eventually settled in Rome after she fell in love with Italian culture. She even learned the language so she could start writing in Italian.

Jhumpa has shown that although everyone battles with loneliness at times, we can all find a place where we truly belong.

BORN: 11 JULY 1967

COUNTRY OF BIRTH: UNITED KINGDOM

NOOR INAYAT KHAN

DARING SECRET AGENT

'LIBERTÉ!'

This cry for freedom was Noor's last word before being executed in a Nazi concentration camp.

Noor was born in Moscow into an aristocratic family – her father was Indian and her mother American. She grew up in London but the family settled in Paris after the First World War, where Noor became a successful children's author and radio presenter.

When the Nazis invaded France in the Second World War, the family fled to the UK. Noor was determined to help win the war, so she decided to volunteer to do one of the most dangerous jobs of all: a secret agent.

After completing her training, Noor was parachuted into France in June 1943. She was the first female wireless operator behind enemy lines! Her mission was to use Morse code to provide resistance fighters in Paris with information to help them defeat the Nazis. Most spies were usually discovered after a few weeks, but remarkably, Noor managed to stay undercover for three months. Sadly, she was eventually betrayed and the Nazis arrested her in October 1943.

Noor was tortured and starved by her captors but refused to reveal any British war secrets. The Nazis saw her as an extraordinarily dangerous spy – she had tried to escape twice! – so they refused to let her interact with other prisoners for fear that she might plot another escape. The formidable spy had survived as a German prisoner of war for nearly a year before being executed in 1944.

Noor's tremendous efforts were recognized with a medal for courage and heroism. Today, a sculpture of her stands in Gordon Square Gardens, London.

BORN: 1 JANUARY 1914   DIED: 13 SEPTEMBER 1944 (AGED 30)
COUNTRY OF BIRTH: RUSSIA

REETA LOI

'THE MORE I AM ME, THE HAPPIER I AM.'

For a long time, Reeta struggled to reconcile her sexual identity with her family's expectations. Since coming out, she has dedicated her life to challenging the negative attitudes faced by other LGBTQ+ South Asians from the wider community. For Reeta, being true to oneself is the best thing one can be.

Reeta's childhood revolved around school, housework, looking after siblings and working in her parents' shop. Her parents grew up with traditional Indian values and imposed the same on their children. Reeta had little freedom. She wasn't allowed to see her friends outside school or talk to boys. Reeta, however, was attracted to girls but was too scared to tell her parents. She turned to drugs and alcohol to cope.

Attending university in London gave Reeta a chance to escape from home. She was finally able to express herself, and even met a girlfriend. But how would her family react when she told them?

Reeta's mother was shocked, while her father was surprisingly accepting. But his attitude changed when Reeta decided to marry her girlfriend – he even threatened to disown his daughter. Reeta was asked to choose between her family and her soulmate. She chose love and married her partner to create the future she wanted.

In 2017, Reeta created the Gaysians network, a place where the UK's gay South Asian community could be themselves and support each other.

Reeta doesn't blame her parents but sees them as victims of a culture and society that have wrongly demonized being gay. Reeta is using her platform to help change these attitudes.

BORN: 9 JUNE 1978

COUNTRY OF BIRTH: UNITED KINGDOM

ILLUSTRATION BY
NAZRINA RODJAN

JAMEELA JAMIL

VOCAL ACTOR

'I JUST CANNOT STAY SILENT ANY MORE.'

Jameela closes her eyes, takes a deep breath and chants these words as she uploads a video of herself fake-crying on the toilet. She's begging people on social media not to buy diet products, insisting they give you painful diarrhoea instead of helping you lose weight.

Born in London to an Indian father and Pakistani mother, Jameela had a lonely childhood. At school she was bullied for her looks, skin colour and for being partially deaf. Jameela developed an eating disorder from all the stress.

When she was seventeen, Jameela was involved in a traumatic car accident that damaged her spine – she wasn't sure she'd ever walk again. This event completely changed Jameela's approach to life and made her fall in love with her body.

After she recovered, Jameela took the bold step to audition to host a music show on UK television. The producers were so impressed by her energy and sense of humour they offered Jameela the job. This role catapulted her to fame. Greater success followed when Jameela moved to the US. Against her own expectations, she was offered a starring role in the hit comedy show, *The Good Place*, and became a global celebrity.

Behind the scenes, Jameela was horrified by the entertainment industry's custom of airbrushing women's photos. She decided to take a stand and only allowed her unedited photos – which included spots on her face and stretchmarks on her bum – to be published. To encourage people to accept and love their bodies, Jameela also founded the inspirational I Weigh movement.

Jameela is using her fame to set a positive example. She encourages people to live life on their own terms and embrace their perceived imperfections.

BORN: 25 FEBRUARY 1986
COUNTRY OF BIRTH: UNITED KINGDOM

ILLUSTRATION BY
SANDEEP JOHAL

KALPANA CHAWLA

PIONEERING ASTRONAUT

'I CHOOSE "KALPANA". IT MEANS "IMAGINATION".'

It was Kalpana's first day at nursery and she had just chosen her own name in front of her teacher and relatives. As the third daughter in her family, Kalpana was determined to show everyone that she wasn't 'just another girl'.

Kalpana was raised in the north Indian city of Karnal. She frequently fell asleep on the roof of her family's home while she gazed at the bright, star-filled sky and fantasized about flying across the heavens and beyond.

Unsurprisingly, she later signed up to study aeronautical engineering at university and was the only woman to do so. Kalpana had gone against her family's wishes – they felt it was more fitting for an Indian woman to become a doctor or teacher.

After graduating in 1982, Kalpana moved to the US and began chasing down her dream of becoming an astronaut. Her first application to the space agency NASA was rejected, but Kalpana kept applying and was eventually accepted. On her first space mission in 1997, she travelled 252 times around the Earth – over 10.4 million miles!

Kalpana flew again in 2003, but tragedy struck – her space shuttle disintegrated upon re-entry into the Earth's atmosphere and the entire crew perished.

The pioneering astronaut who had inspired girls around the world to reach for the stars had lived her life doing what she loved.

Despite often being told 'no' simply because she was a girl, Kalpana persevered and became the first Indian woman to venture into space.

BORN: 17 MARCH 1962   DIED: 1 FEBRUARY 2003 (AGED 40)
COUNTRY OF BIRTH: INDIA

ILLUSTRATION BY
DEEPIKAH R. BHARDWAJ

SANIA MIRZA

ACE TENNIS STAR

'EVERYONE HAS THE RIGHT TO THEIR OPINIONS
AND I HAVE THE RIGHT TO IGNORE THEM.'

When Sania said she wanted to play tennis, her family laughed – she was told girls like her should stay at home and learn to cook. At that moment, Sania knew her journey to the top would be harder because she was a girl. She also knew she would never let that stop her.

The first girl in her family to take up a sport, Sania began playing tennis when she was just six and won her first match two years later. Although still a child, Sania trained up to six hours a day, spending most weekends on the court and travelling across India to play in matches.

At the time, tennis was not popular in India – Sania was ridiculed for enjoying it. Many warned her that if she continued playing tennis in the sun, she would become too dark to ever find a husband!

Wisely, Sania didn't listen and continued to chase her dream. When she won Junior Wimbledon in 2003, her naysayers apologized for their meddling. Since then, she has gone on to win numerous major tournaments.

However, Sania still faces criticism for a range of reasons – from wearing shorts on the tennis court to living with her husband before marriage. She stays focused on what makes her happy and marches to the beat of her own drum.

As the most successful female Indian tennis player in history, Sania is committed to changing attitudes towards women in sports. She uses her influence to inspire and encourage girls to pursue sporting careers, and has founded a tennis academy to make sure there is someone ready to take her place after she retires for good.

BORN: 15 NOVEMBER 1986
COUNTRY OF BIRTH: INDIA

ILLUSTRATION BY
POONAM SAINI

AANCHAL MALHOTRA

PASSIONATE MEMORY COLLECTOR

'I WANT TO GIVE HISTORY A NEW VOICE.'

When British rule in India ended in 1947, the land was divided into two new countries – India and Pakistan – in an event known as the Partition. It was the largest migration in history – over 14 million people had to relocate and up to one million men, women and children died. Aanchal collects fading memories of this time to save them from being lost forever.

Growing up in her grandfather's bookshop in Delhi, Aanchal developed a deep love of books and the tales they contained. She also heard lots of stories from her grandparents, all four of whom had been refugees in the Partition.

Aanchal had little interest in the Partition until one day, in 2013, she started examining two ordinary-looking objects in her family home – a yardstick and a small metal vessel. When her family started to speak about them and their rich history, everything changed for Aanchal.

She realized how ordinary things could unlock stories from the Partition and was inspired to search for more.

Aanchal began talking to former refugees in India, Pakistan and the UK. People became tearful when they showed Aanchal their mementoes and shared their memories – some were uplifting, others sorrowful. Many had never spoken of the past before.

Aanchal encouraged them to write about their experiences, which are shared on her website, Museum of Material Memory. She has also written a book about her discoveries.

Aanchal's efforts have brought together people from around the world and across generations. By collecting their stories, she hopes that the lives of those impacted by one of history's most momentous events are never forgotten.

BORN: 10 JANUARY 1990
COUNTRY OF BIRTH: INDIA

ARUNDHATI ROY

OUTSPOKEN WRITER

'ANOTHER WORLD IS NOT ONLY POSSIBLE, SHE IS ON HER WAY.'

In 1997, Arundhati released her best-selling first novel, *The God of Small Things*, which won the prestigious Booker Prize. Following this success, she could have continued to just write books, earning herself more money and fame. Instead, Arundhati chose to also become an activist, leading from the front and showing how women can create a new, fairer world.

Arundhati's parents divorced when she was aged two. She was raised in Kerala by her mother, a women's rights activist. They had a stormy relationship and, at the age of sixteen, Arundhati moved to Delhi alone to go to university. For a while, she lived in a slum, where she learned first-hand about extreme poverty and how wider society ignored the poor.

After university, Arundhati began to write screenplays for film. In 1992, she began writing her first novel, which took her four years to finish. It was an instant hit and its release catapulted her to international fame.

Eager to make a difference in the world, Arundhati used her new-found fame to become an activist. She campaigned against nuclear weapons that had the power to destroy whole cities, protested to end wars and brought attention to how poor people's lands were being unfairly seized by the Indian government.

Her activism made her powerful enemies, including politicians, corporations and the military. Some tried to scare Arundhati into silence and she was even jailed for refusing to apologize for her actions. None of these struggles deterred Arundhati.

While some say that Arundhati's books and countless awards are her greatest achievement, others believe it is how she helps people who can't stand up for themselves.

BORN: 24 NOVEMBER 1961
COUNTRY OF BIRTH: INDIA

PRITAM KAUR HAYRE

UNSTOPPABLE CHAMPION

'IF SOMEONE NEEDS HELP, I'M THERE.'

On a scorching summer's day on a farm in Cloverdale, Canada, Pritam wiped the sweat from her brow and blew into a horn. It released an earth-shattering blare. Two hundred labourers had been patiently waiting for this moment – Pritam was calling them to gather and protest against their cruel bosses.

Pritam emigrated from India to Canada in 1975 at the age of fifty and began picking berries on local farms. This was a difficult job with long hours and terrible conditions. The workers were poorly paid and didn't have access to toilets or clean drinking water. The job was made even worse by managers forcing the workers to slave away every single day – some workers nearly died!

One day in 1980, after being threatened by a boss at gunpoint, Pritam decided she'd had enough. She resolved to stand up for herself and her co-workers. Pritam led protests and campaigned tirelessly to unite the workers, knowing this was the only way to defeat the bosses. For this, she was fired.

Rather than panicking, Pritam became unstoppable. She fought to get her job back and organized even more protests to demand better working conditions for everyone. Pritam managed to persuade over one hundred berry pickers to join a union and secured better wages and working conditions for everyone. Her hard work had paid off.

Despite not speaking English and having no formal education, Pritam defeated the bosses in court. She even went on to become the Vice-President of the Canadian Farmworkers' Union!

Pritam's remarkable bravery has helped improve the lives of thousands of farmworkers.

BORN: 29 OCTOBER 1925
COUNTRY OF BIRTH: PRESENT-DAY INDIA

ILLUSTRATION BY
SUMAN KAUR

LILLY SINGH

YOUTUBER EXTRAORDINAIRE

'I TOOK THE STAIRS, NOT AN ESCALATOR.'

These words sum up Lilly's tenacious attitude to life and the secret to her success.

Born near Toronto to Punjabi immigrants, Lilly grew up wanting to become an entertainer, but those dreams faded as time passed. After graduating from university, she felt lost and didn't know what she wanted to do. Lilly worked in some tedious jobs that left her feeling depressed. Inspired by a funny clip on YouTube, she decided to make her own video. Although it only received seventy views, this creative expression gave her joy and she decided to make more videos.

Lilly nicknamed herself 'Superwoman' – it made her feel she could overcome any obstacle – and made videos whenever she could. As her following grew, she began to explore everyday issues like racism and sexism using her comedy characters. Her parents encouraged her but set a deadline – Lilly either had to be successful in a year or return to university. So a determined Lilly bought a new camera and got to work, producing as many videos as she could. Her hard work paid off. She gained 100,000 subscribers by the end of that year and began to earn a living from YouTube.

Lilly's videos have now been viewed more than three billion times. She has won several awards and has collaborated with many artists. Lilly has branched out into acting and singing and has her very own show on one of the world's largest television networks, NBC. She uses her popularity to help others by discussing mental health issues and promoting children's rights as a UNICEF ambassador.

To her millions of fans, aka Team Super or Unicorns, she really is a 'bawse'!

BORN: 26 SEPTEMBER 1988
COUNTRY OF BIRTH: CANADA

ILLUSTRATION BY
RAJVINDER KAUR

ANOUSHKA SHANKAR

MUSICAL MAESTRO

'I REALLY WANT TO STEP UP.'

A brilliant musician, Anoushka has won countless awards and is celebrated the world over. When she heard the news that a young Indian woman had been abused and then murdered, Anoushka was hit hard. As a survivor of abuse herself, she felt compelled to lift the veil of silence that continues to affect so many women.

Anoushka comes from a musical family – her father was the famous sitar player, Ravi Shankar, and her half-sister is the singer Norah Jones. From the age of seven, her father became her guru and taught her the sitar, a stringed Indian instrument.

Anoushka quickly became an expert and began touring the world with her father at the age of fourteen. Anoushka developed a unique musical style and just three years later, she released her first

solo album. The accolades soon followed. She was the first Indian artist to perform at the esteemed Grammy Awards.

A turning point came in Anoushka's life when an Indian woman named Jyoti Singh Pandey was killed in Delhi in 2012. It brought back memories of Anoushka's own experiences as a child. Unable to bury these emotions, Anoushka released a powerful video in which she talked about how she had suffered. Anoushka went on to compose a song in Jyoti's name to keep her memory alive and began raising awareness of violence against women.

As well as standing up for victims of abuse, Anoushka has gone on to speak about animal rights, poverty and modern-day slavery. By using her platform and fame, she continues to support others in need of help.

BORN: 9 JUNE 1981
COUNTRY OF BIRTH: UNITED KINGDOM

ILLUSTRATION BY
MEENAL PATEL

SHABANA AZMI

REVOLUTIONARY ACTOR

'ART SHOULD BE USED AS AN INSTRUMENT OF CHANGE.'

Over her forty-year career in Indian and western cinema, Shabana has tackled difficult subjects and shown women in a positive light. Despite attracting criticism for the characters she has played, Shabana has defiantly used her roles to change how women are seen.

Shabana's childhood shaped her ideas about how people should behave. She was raised in a commune in South India where eleven families lived together, sharing all their possessions and responsibilities. This experience taught Shabana about the importance of cooperation. Her mother was an actor and the main breadwinner in the family. Shabana would often be taken to rehearsals at the theatre, which led to a lifelong passion for the arts. Shabana's view of gender equality was heavily influenced by her father, a poet, who often did the household chores.

After graduating from film school, Shabana began to act. After starting her career in theatre, she made her film debut at the age of twenty-four.

At the time, there were strict rules in India over what could be shown on screen. Shabana decided to challenge these ideas, choosing to play strong female characters who were not secondary to men. Her films covered the themes of social injustice and overcoming inequalities. They were often controversial and some even sparked protests. These strong reactions to her work showed Shabana that she had a powerful voice and inspired her to become an activist. She fought for women's rights and campaigned to improve the lives of the poorest in India.

Shabana has used her art to challenge and change the way women are viewed. She continues to strive for a more open-minded and accepting world.

BORN: 18 SEPTEMBER 1950
COUNTRY OF BIRTH: INDIA

ILLUSTRATION BY
POONAM SAINI

ANA

MAHARANI JIND KAUR

REBEL QUEEN

'WEAR THAT, YOU COWARDS! I'LL GO IN TROUSERS AND FIGHT MYSELF!'

An enraged Jind flung her petticoat at a group of fierce Sikh soldiers. They had been fighting the British but were dangerously low on ammunition and close to defeat. Jind's courage wouldn't be enough to save her son's empire.

A few years earlier, Jind's life had been thrown into turmoil. Her husband, Maharaja Ranjit Singh, had died and several heirs to his Sikh Empire were murdered by rivals. Ranjit's youngest son, Duleep Singh, became the maharaja in 1843 at the age of five. Jind was fiercely protective of her son and commandeered the army, ministers and government on his behalf.

When the British declared war against the Sikh Empire in 1845, Jind sent the army into battle but they lost despite her best efforts. The British took over her son's empire but Jind refused to be controlled. Deeply fearing her power,

the British grew increasingly paranoid that she would spark a rebellion Desperate to limit Jind's influence, they imprisoned her. Duleep, aged just nine, was exiled far away from his mother and his homeland.

One night, disguising herself as a servant, Jind made a daring escape from jail. She skilfully evaded capture and travelled over 800 kilometres to seek refuge in Nepal.

Jind and Duleep were finally reunited in 1861 after being separated for thirteen years. She moved to England to be with her son. Despite her failing health, the shrewd queen saw her final opportunity to strike at the British. Before she died, Jind reminded Duleep about his lost kingdom and begged him to reclaim his throne. Inspired by his mother's words, Duleep would rebel against the British. Even in death, Jind remained a thorn in the British Empire's side.

BORN: 1817   DIED: 1 AUGUST 1863 (AGED 46)
COUNTRY OF BIRTH: PRESENT-DAY PAKISTAN

ILLUSTRATION BY
DEEPIKAH R. BHARDWAJ

MEERA SYAL

CREATIVE POWERHOUSE

'FITTING IN MEANT FORGETTING WHO I WAS.'

As a child, Meera was so desperate to fit in that she often wished for blonde hair and an English name. In time, she would embrace her heritage and make it cool to be a British Asian.

Growing up, Meera felt like an outsider as hers was the only Indian family in their little English mining village near Wolverhampton. Meera spent her teenage years feeling unhappy and self-conscious about her weight and appearance. She coped by telling jokes, which also helped others better understand her.

Meera always dreamed of doing something creative – as a child she took great joy in writing plays and having friends act out the roles. She didn't know exactly what to do but the thought of getting a normal job terrified her. So she studied drama and English at university and realized that being different made her unique and interesting.

Meera stopped trying to fit in and instead began to use elements of her culture and identity in her writing and acting.

Meera was living her dream – she was acting on television and writing screenplays for films. Huge success followed when she co-wrote and starred in *Goodness Gracious Me*, a groundbreaking comedy that challenged British and South Asian stereotypes. British Asians related to the show's many characters, helping them fuse their Asian culture with their British upbringing.

Meera has been able to use her incredible creative talents to perform in major theatre productions, star in hit television shows and write award-winning books.

By not fitting in, she has helped British Asians celebrate their culture while entertaining everyone along the way.

BORN: 27 JUNE 1961

COUNTRY OF BIRTH: UNITED KINGDOM

NEELAM GILL

RESILIENT MODEL

'I HATED MY SKIN COLOUR BECAUSE I THOUGHT BEING LIGHTER WAS WHAT WAS BEAUTIFUL.'

Battling against colourism and body-shaming, Neelam took the fashion industry by storm to become one of the world's top models.

Neelam was raised in a rough part of Coventry. Her difficult childhood was made worse by her parents' divorce and racist bullying at school. She was ridiculed daily for her body shape, looks and dark complexion. Neelam became ashamed of her skin colour and would avoid the sun for fear of becoming darker. Even other South Asians criticized her skin colour. A modelling agency scout spotted Neelam when she was fourteen. Her mother agreed to let her model, but only after completing school. Four years later, Neelam left school with exceptional grades and started building her modelling portfolio.

The global fashion brand Burberry invited Neelam to their offices in London. She was excited but couldn't afford the train ticket and didn't go. Burberry invited her again a week later and this time Neelam scraped the money together. After meeting her, Burberry were so impressed they asked Neelam to model in one of their upcoming campaigns. She accepted and became the first person of Indian heritage to model for them. But behind the scenes Neelam was being abused online for her complexion and ethnicity. She responded by posting a video on YouTube discussing bullying, mental health and self-worth. The video reached thousands and Neelam now speaks frequently about these issues.

Neelam has gone on to model for some of the biggest global brands. By standing tall in the face of adversity over her own appearance, she continues to show there is more than just one kind of beauty.

BORN: 27 APRIL 1995
COUNTRY OF BIRTH: UNITED KINGDOM

AMRITA SHER-GIL

ILLUSTRIOUS ARTIST

'SOMETHING VITAL, CONNECTED WITH THE SOIL,
SOMETHING ESSENTIALLY INDIAN.'

Amrita was a revolutionary painter who changed the way Indians were portrayed in art. Going against the trend of painting stereotypical scenes of the joyous Indian life enjoyed by the rich, she chose instead to portray the ordinary and the humble.

Amrita was born in Budapest to a Hungarian opera singer and Indian scholar and aristocrat. The family moved to India when Amrita was eight. She was a creative child and was given lessons in different painting methods. Amrita would often draw pictures of her toys or write colourfully illustrated fairy tales.

An uncle who saw Amrita's ability taught her drawing techniques and encouraged her to take her art more seriously. At age sixteen, Amrita's parents took her to Paris to train at an art school where many great European artists had studied. There Amrita flourished and her painting style matured considerably.

Amrita soon came to be regarded as an artistic sensation – not only was she extraordinarily talented, she was also remarkably young. Despite her growing fame, Amrita longed to go back to India. She returned to India in 1934 and found herself forever changed. Her visit made clear her true purpose – to capture on her canvas the daily difficulties faced by normal, poor Indians, especially women, so others could better appreciate their daily existence.

Amrita died unexpectedly at the height of her career. Described as one of the most innovative artists of the 20th century, Amrita is widely recognized as the mother of modern art in India. Passionate to the last, she is rumoured to have spent her final breaths murmuring about colours.

BORN: 30 JANUARY 1913   DIED: 5 DECEMBER 1941 (AGED 28)
COUNTRY OF BIRTH: HUNGARY

ILLUSTRATION BY
SANDEEP JOHAL

MIRA NAIR

ACCLAIMED FILMMAKER

'IF WE DON'T TELL OUR OWN STORIES, NO ONE ELSE WILL.'

Before the Internet Age, South Asian documentary filmmakers like Mira had few opportunities to show their work on screen. Mira realized she needed to change her approach to storytelling if she was going to get her work seen.

Raised and educated in India, Mira went to the US to study. It was there that she became fascinated with the power of filmmaking and made her first major documentary about an Indian immigrant living in 1980s America. She continued to explore her passion, directing and producing several award-winning documentaries. However, faced with limited audience numbers, Mira resolved to take on a new challenge and make a feature film.

In 1988, Mira co-wrote a film screenplay called *Salaam Bombay!* about the day-to-day lives of children living in the slums of India's biggest city. A UK production company was keen to support the project, but only if Mira could raise fifty per cent of the money to make it. She failed to reach this target, but told the production company that she had succeeded!

When filming began, Mira took the bold decision to film real street children rather than use actors. After filming had ended, she ensured the children received an education and other support. The film was a huge success, won countless awards and was even nominated for an Oscar.

Mira has gone on to make several other acclaimed films. She has won many awards, including the most coveted award at the Venice Film Festival for her film *Monsoon Wedding*, one of only a handful of women to ever have done so. Mira's authentic stories continue to excite and inspire people across the world.

BORN: 15 OCTOBER 1957

COUNTRY OF BIRTH: INDIA

ILLUSTRATION BY
ANU CHOUHAN

RUPI KAUR

RECORD-BREAKING POET

'TAKE THESE SIMPLE WORDS AND
CREATE SOMETHING THAT TOUCHES YOU.'

Through her poems on the themes of trauma and healing, love and femininity, Rupi touches the lives of many young women around the world.

Rupi was born in Punjab, North India, and migrated to Canada at the age of four with her family. As she couldn't speak English, her mother encouraged her to draw and paint, which became her first passions.

Rupi started writing poetry for friends at school before performing her work on stage at the age of seventeen. She was inspired by writers like Khalil Gibran, who created powerful imagery using simple words. Rupi began to post her work on Instagram, where her mixture of poetry and hand-drawn illustrations attracted a large following. However, when she tried to publish her poems in a book, a university professor discouraged her, telling her that no one buys poetry books, especially those written by Indian women.

Undeterred, she decided to self-publish her first book, *Milk and Honey*, in 2014. A few months later, Rupi posted an image of herself in period-stained pyjamas on Instagram for a university assignment. Though periods are perfectly natural, the picture was removed by Instagram moderators for being offensive. Bitterly disappointed, Rupi campaigned to have the photo reposted, gaining global attention.

After this controversy, Rupi's book was quickly picked up by a publisher who was impressed with her thought-provoking messages.

Milk and Honey soon became a smash hit. It topped *The New York Times* Best Seller list for over a year, sold over 5 million copies and has been translated into more than 45 languages!

Rupi followed up on this success with a second collection of poetry, *The Sun and Her Flowers*, and continues to inspire millions.

BORN: 4 OCTOBER 1992
COUNTRY OF BIRTH: INDIA

SOPHIA DULEEP SINGH

FEISTY SUFFRAGETTE

'GIVE WOMEN THE VOTE!'

Brandishing a banner bearing this simple slogan, Sophia hurled herself at the British prime minister's car. She was demanding that women be treated equally to men.

Sophia was raised at a stately house in Suffolk. Her father was Maharaja Duleep Singh, the exiled king of the Sikh Empire. Sophia's German-Ethiopian mother died when she was ten and her godmother, Queen Victoria, took responsibility for her upbringing. Sophia was educated, attended balls at Buckingham Palace and given a flat at Hampton Court Palace.

The media followed the celebrity princess with interest. They loved her style and her exotic dogs and often photographed her cycling – she was one of the first women to do so in public! But a trip to India changed everything.

Although forbidden to travel, Sophia journeyed in secret to India in 1903. She was shocked by the extreme poverty and racism suffered by Indians at the hands of the British. She vowed to make a difference.

Back in England, the fight for women's rights caught Sophia's eye. She became a suffragette in 1909 and began protesting in the streets and fundraising for the movement. Sophia knew the media couldn't resist talking about her and used this to raise awareness about the fight for women's rights. Thousands learned about the suffragettes through the widespread publicity Sophia received. The government was at a loss – even a frustrated King George V remarked, 'Have we no hold on her?'

The outbreak of the First World War didn't slow Sophia down – she fought for women to work and nursed wounded soldiers.

Women were finally allowed to vote in 1918. Despite making enemies of powerful men, Sophia's deeds changed the lives of women forever.

BORN: 8 AUGUST 1876   DIED: 22 AUGUST 1948 (AGED 72)
COUNTRY OF BIRTH: UNITED KINGDOM

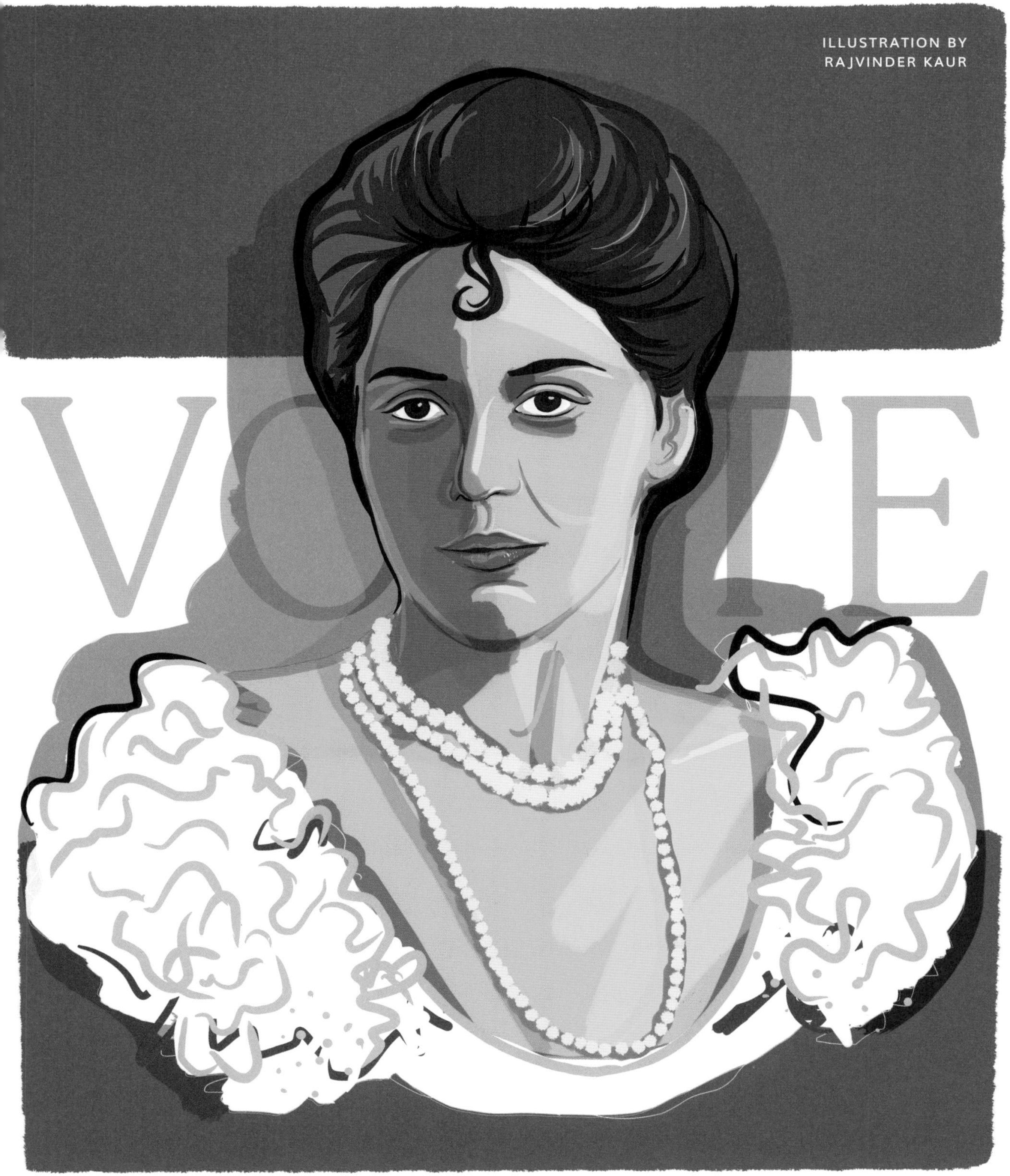

ILLUSTRATION BY
RAJVINDER KAUR

KARPAL KAUR SANDHU

PIONEERING POLICE OFFICER

'BEING A POLICE OFFICER ISN'T LADYLIKE!'

Karpal longed to join the police but her husband was against it, insisting it wasn't a woman's job. She ignored him and went on to become the world's first South Asian female police officer.

Karpal moved to England from Zanzibar in 1962 when she got a job as a nurse. Racist violence in the UK was on the rise and life was becoming increasingly dangerous for South Asians and other ethnic minorities. Many people suffered discrimination at the hands of the police, who often refused to investigate racist attacks. Some police officers were guilty of racial harassment and violence themselves.

In this climate, Karpal faced strong opposition to her goal of joining the police force from her husband, family and wider community. Karpal refused to be swayed – she was determined to do whatever she could to make the UK a better place to live.

Karpal's dream came true in 1971 when she joined the London Metropolitan Police. She worked extremely hard assisting in criminal investigations, patrolling the streets and acting as an interpreter.

Karpal's exceptional work drew praise from her senior officers who valued how her energy and intelligence helped bridge the gap between the police and immigrant communities.

Tragically, Karpal's promising career was cut short by her untimely death.

Although she had only served as a police officer for two years, Karpal blazed a trail that has since been followed by hundreds of South Asian female police officers across the UK.

BORN: 1943   DIED: 4 NOVEMBER 1973 (AGED 30)
COUNTRY OF BIRTH: PRESENT-DAY TANZANIA

ILLUSTRATION BY
SANDEEP JOHAL

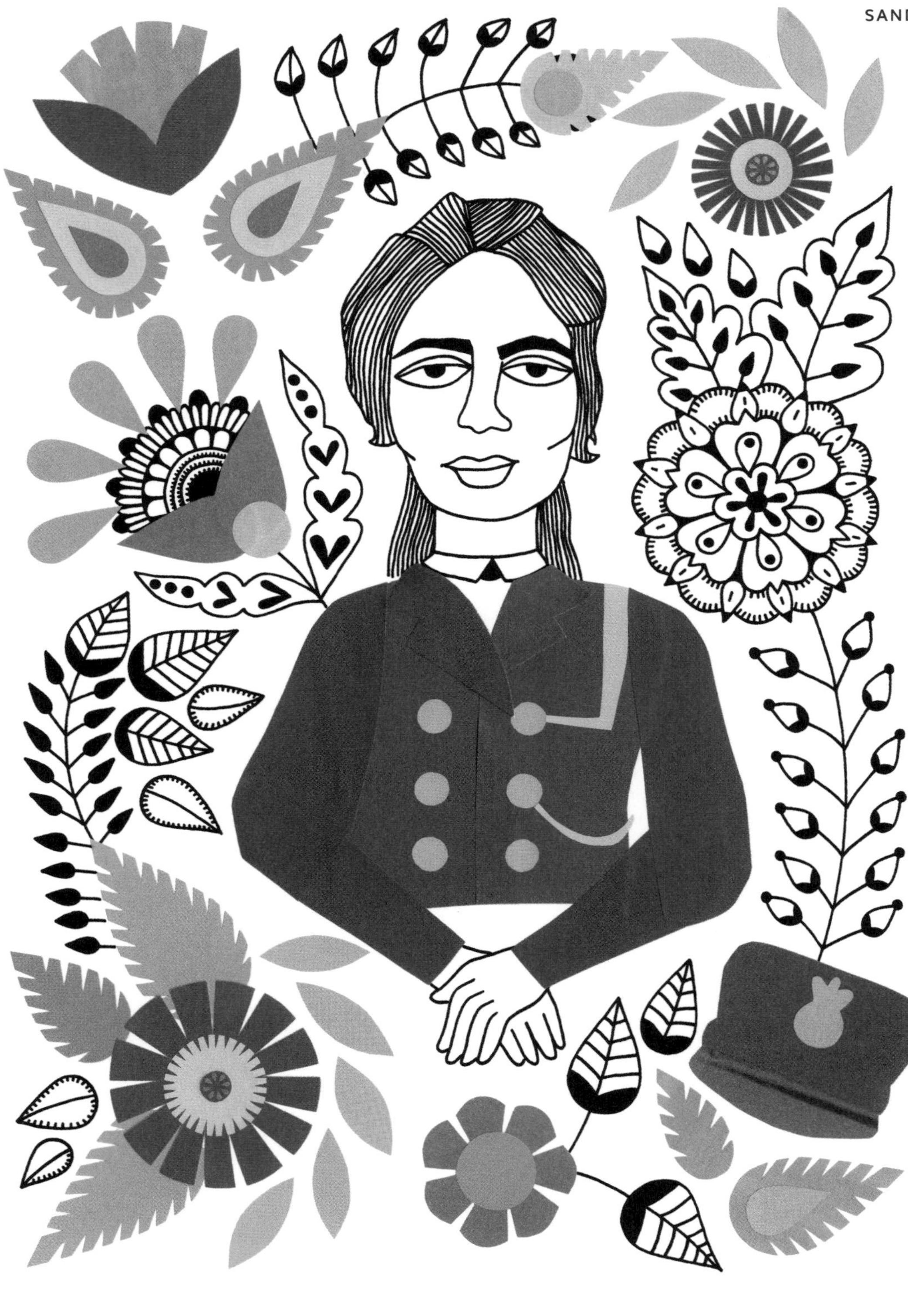

SHARMEEN OBAID-CHINOY

VOICE OF THE OPPRESSED

'SPEAK THE TRUTH AND I WILL STAND WITH YOU.'

Sharmeen's father offered her unwavering support despite their recent misfortune – their home had been vandalized by local bullies after an article Sharmeen wrote exposed their bad behaviour. Taking inspiration from her father's words, she would use her talents to provide a voice and audience for those who go unheard.

One of five sisters born in Karachi, Sharmeen was an outspoken child – she would not hesitate to tell off anyone offering condolences to her mother for having so many daughters. Sharmeen was also known for sticking up for herself and others. When a friend suggested she channel her passion into writing, Sharmeen listened. By fourteen, Sharmeen had written her first article, which was featured in a national newspaper. This was the beginning of her career as a spokesperson for the oppressed.

Sharmeen worked as a journalist for the remainder of her teens, writing about human rights issues and investigating corrupt politicians.

While studying in the US, Sharmeen wrote an article about how Afghan child refugees were living on the streets of Pakistan because of the American invasion of Afghanistan in 2001. She was desperate to share the children's experiences in a documentary but, with no experience in filmmaking, she struggled to find a producer. Her proposal was eventually accepted by *The New York Times*. After a crash-course in filmmaking, Sharmeen headed to Pakistan to collect the children's stories. Their interviews became her first documentary, *Terror's Children*.

Sharmeen has gone on to make over ten more documentaries focusing mainly on human rights and gender issues. She has won many major awards and in 2021 she is the only South Asian woman to have won two Oscars.

BORN: 12 NOVEMBER 1978
COUNTRY OF BIRTH: PAKISTAN

ILLUSTRATION BY
VINNY SOOR

TIA KANSARA

'THE EARTH IS A BODY THAT ALSO NEEDS NOURISHING.'

Tia has many talents and could have chosen any career. But once she learned about the poor health of our planet, she decided to try to save the world.

It was at home in Birmingham that Tia's Gujarati parents first taught her the importance of respecting nature and not wasting food. Tia loved being outdoors and when she volunteered to help restore Birmingham's canals at the age of thirteen, the need to protect the environment hit home.

Tia wanted a career with a purpose that matched her values, not just a job. After university, she happened to meet with an architect and began working at his company in 2008. On her first big project, Tia went to Costa Rica to give a talk on the idea of sustainability, which ensures future generations can enjoy the same natural resources we use today.

Realizing time was running out to reverse the damage we've done to the air, land and sea, Tia devoted the next six years to researching solutions to environmental problems.

She learned about the Earth's skyrocketing population, how pollution and waste are damaging the planet, and the risk of natural resources running out.

Tia soon became an expert on designing cities of the future that could create healthy communities and nourish Mother Earth. She shared her ideas on how we can make a positive contribution to nature by combining the power of technology and community in her book, *Replenish*, which became a best-seller.

By sharing her findings with individuals, communities, businesses and governments around the world, Tia is helping everyone understand how they can help heal our planet.

BORN: 19 APRIL 1983
COUNTRY OF BIRTH: UNITED KINGDOM

ILLUSTRATION BY
KOKILA BHATTACHARYA

JHANSI KI RANI

WARRIOR QUEEN

'I WILL NOT GIVE UP MY KINGDOM!'

It was 1854 and Rani Lakshmi Bai's husband, the ruler of Jhansi, had recently died. She expected her adopted son to become the new king, but the British rulers in India refused to recognize him as a legitimate heir. According to their rules, he could not be king, so they swiftly took over the kingdom. The British ignored Lakshmi Bai's appeals for justice and forced her out of her palace.

Lakshmi Bai was raised by her father after her mother's untimely death. She learned how to shoot a gun, fire arrows and ride her horse with a sword in each hand and the reins gripped between her teeth. Lakshmi Bai later married the king of Jhansi, a small state in northern India making her Jhansi ki Rani, the queen of Jhansi. In 1851, their baby son tragically died, so they adopted the king's nephew.

A few years after Lakshmi Bai had lost her kingdom, rebellions broke out across India when Indian soldiers revolted against British rule. The fighting eventually reached Jhansi. Rebels killed the kingdom's small British population and Lakshmi Bai was blamed even though she wasn't involved. Soon after, two neighbouring kings attacked Jhansi. Lakshmi Bai begged the British to send reinforcements – she needed to protect her people yet had no army – but they refused. Left with no other choice, she turned to the rebels for assistance.

Lakshmi Bai's alliance with the rebels infuriated the British and they responded by besieging Jhansi and bombarding the fort. Despite valiant resistance, she was forced to flee. In a desperate last stand, Lakshmi Bai fought courageously on horseback alongside her soldiers and was fatally wounded. This heroic leader's legacy would live on in the fight for India's independence.

BORN: 19 NOVEMBER 1828   DIED: 18 JUNE 1858 (AGED 29)
COUNTRY OF BIRTH: PRESENT-DAY INDIA

ILLUSTRATION BY
ANU CHOUHAN

MINDY KALING

COMEDY CREATIVE

'IT'S SO WEIRD BEING MY OWN ROLE MODEL.'

Starring in the popular television show *The Office* gave Mindy the chance to show American audiences what it meant to be South Asian. Having had no one like her to look up to when she was breaking into the entertainment industry, Mindy is determined to pave a path for others to follow.

As a child, Mindy loved how her mother made people laugh. She dreamed of becoming a comedy writer so that she too could do the same. Mindy studied playwriting at university, hoping it would help her accomplish her goal. Her first taste of success came when she published a comic strip filled with dark, witty humour in the university newspaper.

After graduating, Mindy worked as an intern on a big American chat show. Realizing that families like hers were never shown on television, Mindy started writing and performing her own comedy scripts. When the creator of *The Office* saw her performing one day, he was impressed. He hired Mindy as the first female writer on the show. She also acted in it and won a number of awards for her hilarious performances as Kelly Kapoor.

Mindy went on to write and produce her own comedy show about the life of an Indian-American woman called, *The Mindy Project*. It was the first show by a person of Indian heritage on American television and was another great success. The multi-talented Mindy has starred in other television shows and movies, and even written best-selling books.

As a creative force, Mindy is representing her culture in a positive way. She has broken barriers for young South Asians to pursue careers that they might never have previously considered.

BORN: 24 JUNE 1979

COUNTRY OF BIRTH: UNITED STATES OF AMERICA

ILLUSTRATION BY
RAJVINDER KAUR

RAVINDER BHOGAL

MASTER CHEF

'I COOK THE FOOD OF IMMIGRANTS.'

After Ravinder's family moved to Kent from Nairobi, Friday night became 'English Food Night'. Her mother would take traditional British cuisine and add Indian and Kenyan touches. Ravinder didn't know it then, but her mother's fusion dishes would shape her unique cooking style.

When Ravinder was five, her grandfather bought her a child-sized stove to inspire her to cook. Although the things she cooked were often burned or flavourless, her grandfather ate them enthusiastically, showering her with praise. Ravinder began to fall in love with cooking.

A few years later, Ravinder's mother began teaching her how to cook. Ravinder quickly moved on to helping her mother prepare Friday night meals. Cooking became one of Ravinder's favourite pastimes.

Ravinder didn't think she could make a living as a chef, so after university she pursued a career in fashion journalism.

She continued cooking as a hobby, often taking delicious home-cooked treats to share with her work colleagues.

In 2007, a friend told Ravinder about a new television cooking competition – Gordon Ramsay, one of the world's most famous chefs, was looking for the next big cooking star. Ravinder applied and beat 9,000 contestants when she was crowned the winner. She became a rising culinary star and life as she knew it was about to change completely.

Ravinder went on to release an award-winning book, present television shows and open a restaurant in London.

Like her mother did so many years before, Ravinder is known for taking traditional dishes and infusing them with other aspects of her Kenyan, Indian, Persian and British heritage. She is a pioneer of fusion cuisine.

BORN: 9 MAY 1978
COUNTRY OF BIRTH: KENYA

ILLUSTRATION BY
POONAM SAINI

IMTIAZ DHARKER

ARTISTIC POET

'POETRY IS A WAY OF SAYING THINGS WHICH WOULD BE DIFFICULT FOR OTHERS TO SAY.'

Imtiaz's powerful poems draw on her own experiences of living in Pakistan, Scotland and India. Covering themes of childhood, borders, journeys and freedom, her poetry reaches out and touches those who have ever felt lost.

As a child, Imtiaz moved from Lahore to Glasgow, where she grew up surrounded by a large South Asian community.

At university, she met and fell in love with her future husband and, after graduating, they both relocated to Mumbai.

Mumbai was a completely different world from Glasgow. Imtiaz saw extreme poverty, discrimination against women and tension between different religious groups, which opened her mind to the lives of those much less fortunate than her.

Imtiaz began expressing what she saw first through pen-and-ink drawings and then later through poetry. Her first collection of poems discussed the impact of culture, honour and societal expectations on women's lives and was published in a book called *Purdah* ('Veil').

Since then, Imtiaz has written many other inspirational poetry collections. She has also produced over 200 documentary films, covering issues of belonging, identity and power, and she has won several prestigious awards for her work.

Imtiaz's work now features on UK school curricula and is taught to countless young adults every year.

Through her work, Imtiaz continues to shed light on the obstacles standing in the way of women and girls around the world.

BORN: 31 JANUARY 1954
COUNTRY OF BIRTH: PAKISTAN

ILLUSTRATION BY
DEEPIKAH R. BHARDWAJ

JAYABEN DESAI

FEARLESS PROTESTER

'WHAT YOU ARE RUNNING HERE IS NOT A FACTORY, IT IS A ZOO!'

Her eyes ablaze, Jayaben stormed out of the factory with nearly one hundred co-workers behind her. Unknown to her, she had just begun one of the largest workers' protests in British history.

Jayaben was born in the Indian state of Gujarat in 1933 but settled in Tanzania in East Africa after marriage. Her comfortable lifestyle ended abruptly in the early 1970s when political changes swept across Africa and forced Indians to flee to the UK.

She joined other South Asian women at the Grunwick factory in London. Black and Asian workers typically worked the lowest-paid jobs and often earned less than their white colleagues. They worked punishingly long hours in dreadful conditions and faced continual harassment and bullying. Jayaben decided to take a stand.

When Jayaben marched out of the factory that day in 1976, she organized a strike and joined a union. She then visited over 1,000 workplaces, including engineering factories in Scotland and coal mines in Wales, encouraging others to fight with her to improve their own working conditions.

Despite the arrests of Jayaben's co-workers and opposition from some men in their families, support for the 'strikers in saris' (as the press called them) skyrocketed to more than 20,000 people from across the UK.

Finally, after two years of fighting, the workers lost a court case and had to concede defeat. But by bringing people together to defend workers' rights, Jayaben's actions shattered stereotypes of South Asian women as feeble and powerless.

BORN: 2 APRIL 1933   DIED: 23 DECEMBER 2010 (AGED 77)
COUNTRY OF BIRTH: PRESENT-DAY INDIA

ILLUSTRATION BY
SANDEEP JOHAL

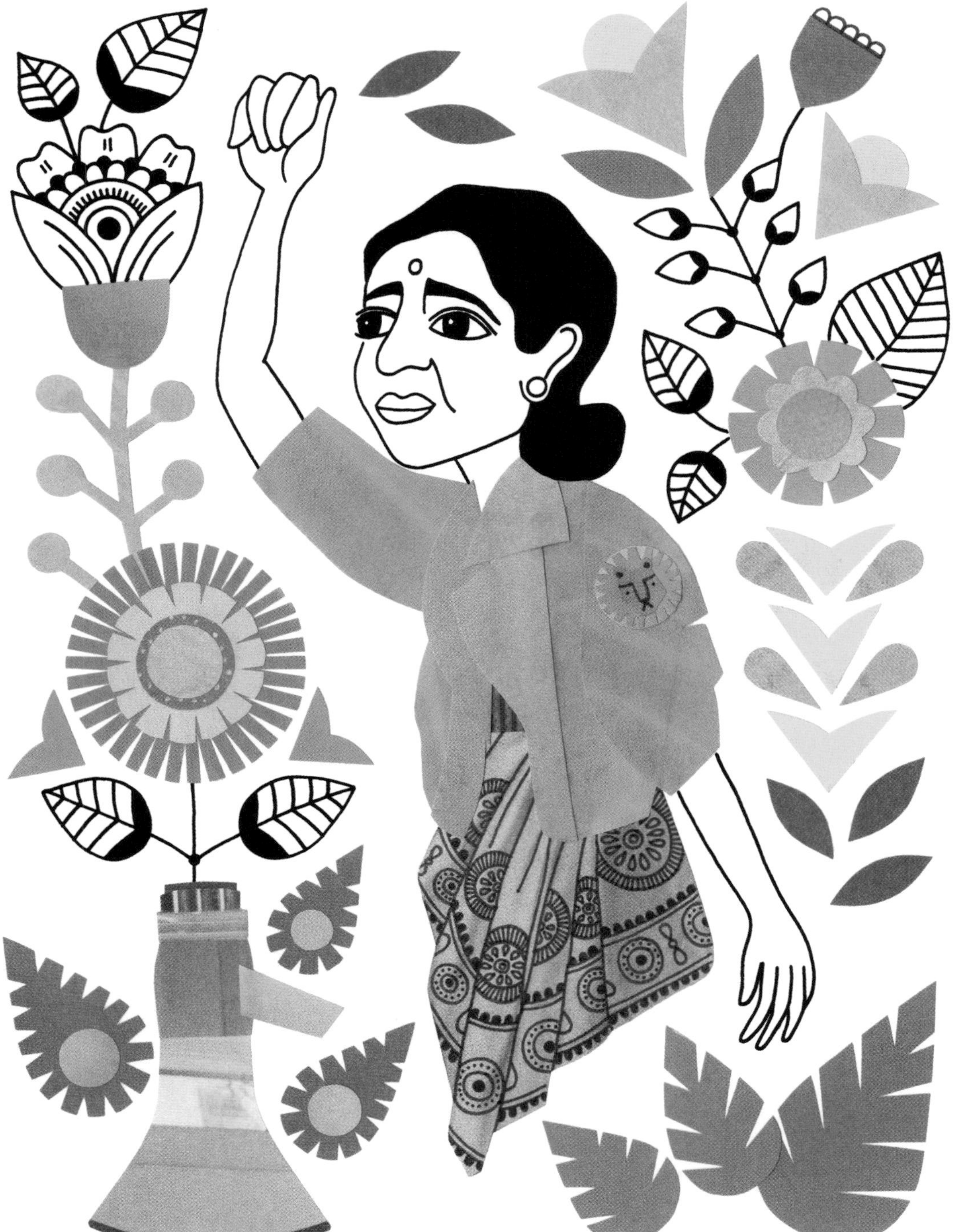

SHAINA AZAD

GO-GETTING ENTREPRENEUR

'IF YOU WORK HARD AND STAY HUMBLE, THE SKY'S THE LIMIT.'

This is Shaina's advice to anyone aspiring to achieve her success.

Shaina loved art and painting as a child. Her passion for colours developed into a love for make-up art after she volunteered to do the actors' make-up for a school play. Everyone, including Shaina, was delighted with her work.

Shaina maintained her passion for make-up throughout university and even while working as a journalist in Egypt – after a busy working week she would spend weekends refining her artistry on Egyptian brides. Shaina loved journalism but realized her heart was in make-up artistry.

Determined to pursue this new career, Shaina returned to Canada. She launched her own YouTube channel to showcase her skills. She began freelancing as a bridal make-up artist and did the make-up for actors on local television and film sets. Shaina was fired up – she attended as

many events as she could to meet expert make-up artists from the film, music and fashion industries, even offering to clean their brushes so she could get close to the artists to learn from them.

As Shaina's online presence grew, she was spotted by a major American television channel – they wanted her to discuss the cosmetics industry on one of their most popular shows. She loved the experience and decided to create her own make-up line.

After many sleepless nights spent researching and testing ingredients for her products, Shaina finally launched SUVA Beauty in 2015 from her home. Initially offering just a handful of products, demand soared and Shaina went on to create nearly eighty more products – including a special brush case that she invented.

What started out as a girl in her living room is now a brand that retails in over thirty countries.

BORN: 16 JUNE 1986
COUNTRY OF BIRTH: CANADA

NORAH JONES

SENSATIONAL SINGER

'I DON'T TRY TO SOUND LIKE ANYONE BUT ME.'

When Norah released her first album, she felt hopeful that people would like it. Little did she know that it would become one of the biggest-selling debut albums of all time.

Norah was born into a musical family. Her American mother was a concert producer and her Indian father a world-famous classical musician. When Norah's parents split up, she was raised by her mother. As a child, Norah would often listen to her mother's records, which sparked a lifelong love for different kinds of music. She learned how to play a range of instruments and won awards for her performances at school, which gave her the confidence to pursue a career in music.

After studying piano at university, Norah moved to New York where she sang in local clubs. She caught the attention of a record label but they weren't sure whether her unique blend of jazz, blues and folk music would be popular. However, when they saw her perform, they were amazed and gave her a record deal.

At the age of twenty-two, Norah released Come Away With Me, her first album. One of the songs 'Don't Know Why' was a huge radio hit and the album quickly soared to the top of the charts. Norah became the second best-selling debut artist of all time, with album sales of over 27 million worldwide. Her extraordinary style was also a hit with people in the music industry, who voted for her to win an incredible six Grammys at her first music awards ceremony.

With over 50 million albums sold, Norah continues to do what she loves most – to push the boundaries of her musical talent to reach out to people everywhere.

BORN: 30 MARCH 1979

COUNTRY OF BIRTH: UNITED STATES OF AMERICA

ILLUSTRATION BY
MEENAL PATEL

RAZIA SULTAN

DEFIANT MONARCH

'IF I DON'T PROVE TO BE BETTER THAN A MAN, YOU MAY CUT MY HEAD OFF.'

Razia's words echoed across the mosque as she addressed the people of Delhi. She was asking them to honour her late father's wishes and make her their sultan.

When Razia was a child, her father, the Sultan of Delhi, often left her in charge of the government when he went travelling. She proved so capable during these periods that the sultan decreed Razia would be his successor instead of her brothers.

When the sultan died in 1236 his advisers could not bear the idea of a woman in charge. So they defied the sultan's wishes and crowned Razia's brother, Rukn-ud-Din, instead. Heartbroken, Razia appealed to the people for justice. They were so moved by her plea that they stormed the royal palace, imprisoned her brother and made her their ruler.

Razia proved to be a fair and intelligent monarch who cared for all her subjects.

She set up an efficient system of law and order, encouraged trade and established education centres. Despite this, her father's advisers still disliked her. They hated that Razia acted without consulting them, wore men's clothing and insisted on being called sultan rather than sultana.

When a nearby governor, Malik Altunia, rose up against Razia, the advisers began plotting against her. As she rode into battle against Altunia, the advisers mutinied and Razia was captured. Taking advantage of Razia's absence, the advisers returned to Delhi and enthroned her brother, Bahrum Shah. Razia cleverly convinced Altunia to help her reclaim her kingdom. He agreed and together they attacked Bahrum Shah. Sadly, Razia was defeated and executed the next day.

In the end, the first female ruler in India was defeated by those who couldn't accept a woman as their sultan.

BORN: 1205   DIED: 14 OCTOBER 1240 (AGED 35)
COUNTRY OF BIRTH: PRESENT-DAY INDIA

ILLUSTRATION BY
VINNY SOOR

GAZAL DHALIWAL

TRAILBLAZING TRANSWOMAN

'ALWAYS REMEMBER, YOU ARE NOT ALONE.'

This is Gazal's advice to people who are worried about telling the world who they really are.

Gazal was raised in Punjab as a boy named Gunraj. Gazal tried hard to fit in with boys, but knew she was different. No one understood how she felt, including her own parents. This often left her feeling isolated and alone. She would later learn that she was suffering with gender dysphoria and that there were thousands of others who felt just like she did.

Gazal continued to live as a man through university. When she started her first job, Gazal hated it – denying who she really was led to depression, and Gazal realized that she was living a lie. Eventually, Gazal summoned the courage and turned to her parents. Although it was hard for them to understand her struggle, they just wanted her to be happy. They supported Gazal when she changed her name and began living as a woman.

A weight had been lifted from Gazal's shoulders and she felt free to pursue her passion to become a screenwriter.

In 2009, she moved to Mumbai, the heart of the Bollywood film industry. Her big break came when she wrote the mainstream Indian film *Ek Ladki Ko Dekha Toh Aisa Laga* ('How I Felt When I Saw That Girl'). The film was about an Indian girl telling her family she is gay and starred some of Bollywood's biggest actors. It was a super-hit and many have said that this film would help anyone struggling to accept their own sexual identity.

Gazal has used her own challenging experiences to bring LGBTQ+ stories into mainstream Indian cinema.

BORN: 1982
COUNTRY OF BIRTH: INDIA

ILLUSTRATION BY
NAZRINA RODJAN

INDRA NOOYI

BRILLIANT BUSINESSWOMAN

'BE YOURSELF.'

This was the advice given to Indra by her university professor. Indra would be guided by these words for the rest of her career, which would see her reach the top of one of the world's largest and most recognized food and beverage brands.

Growing up in Chennai, Indra often defied social conventions. As a child, she was a guitarist in an all-girl rock band and a keen cricket player. When she was accepted onto a master's degree course at Yale, one of the most prestigious universities in the world, her mother wanted her to stay in India and get married. With her father's backing, Indra moved to the US to pursue her education.

Even though she received a full scholarship, Indra still had to work to make ends meet. When she was invited to interview for an exciting summer job,

Indra faced a dilemma – she couldn't afford a business suit. Remembering her professor's advice, she decided to just be herself and wore a sari to the interview. She got the job, and so began her remarkable journey.

Indra joined PepsiCo in 1994 as a strategic leader and quickly made a name for herself as an expert on business deals. After she accomplished one of the biggest food deals in history, Indra was rewarded with the top job, becoming PepsiCo's first-ever female chief executive officer (CEO) in 2001.

Awarded first place on *Fortune* magazine's Most Powerful Women list for five years in a row, Indra has been recognized as one of the best CEOs and most influential people in the world.

BORN: 28 OCTOBER 1955
COUNTRY OF BIRTH: INDIA

ILLUSTRATION BY
KOKILA BHATTACHARYA

SANA AMANAT

MARVELLOUS COMIC-BOOK CREATOR

'I WANT TO TELL A DIFFERENT KIND OF STORY.'

When Sana created a comic-book character based on her experiences of growing up feeling like an outsider, she did something extraordinary.

Raised in New Jersey, Sana felt like she didn't fit in because her parents were Muslim immigrants from Pakistan. This was made worse by the fact that she rarely saw people who looked like her on television or in books and films.

After the terrorist attacks in New York on 11 September 2001, there was a great deal of anti-Muslim feeling across the US. Some of Sana's classmates made her feel ashamed of her identity. Feeling isolated, Sana found comfort in comic-books. She was especially touched by the X-Men series – she loved the underlying messages of accepting others and learning from people of different backgrounds. These powerful ideas would later inspire Sana's own comic-book creation.

After university, Sana worked in magazine publishing. She then joined a small comic-book company where she mastered the art of storytelling. Soon after, Sana was approached by Marvel Comics who asked her to join their team. They believed that Sana's fresh voice and new ideas could help Marvel to connect with more readers. She helped to create the first female Muslim superhero – Kamala Khan, aka Ms Marvel. Inspired by elements from Sana's life, Kamala is a teenage Pakistani-American from New Jersey who has the power to change her shape.

The comic-book was a hit with many people around the world, winning awards and making *The New York Times* Best Seller list. Sana's vision to create a character with whom women and girls of all backgrounds could connect, especially those struggling with their identity, was a super-powered success!

BORN: 22 JUNE 1982
COUNTRY OF BIRTH: UNITED STATES OF AMERICA

ILLUSTRATION BY
VINNY SOOR

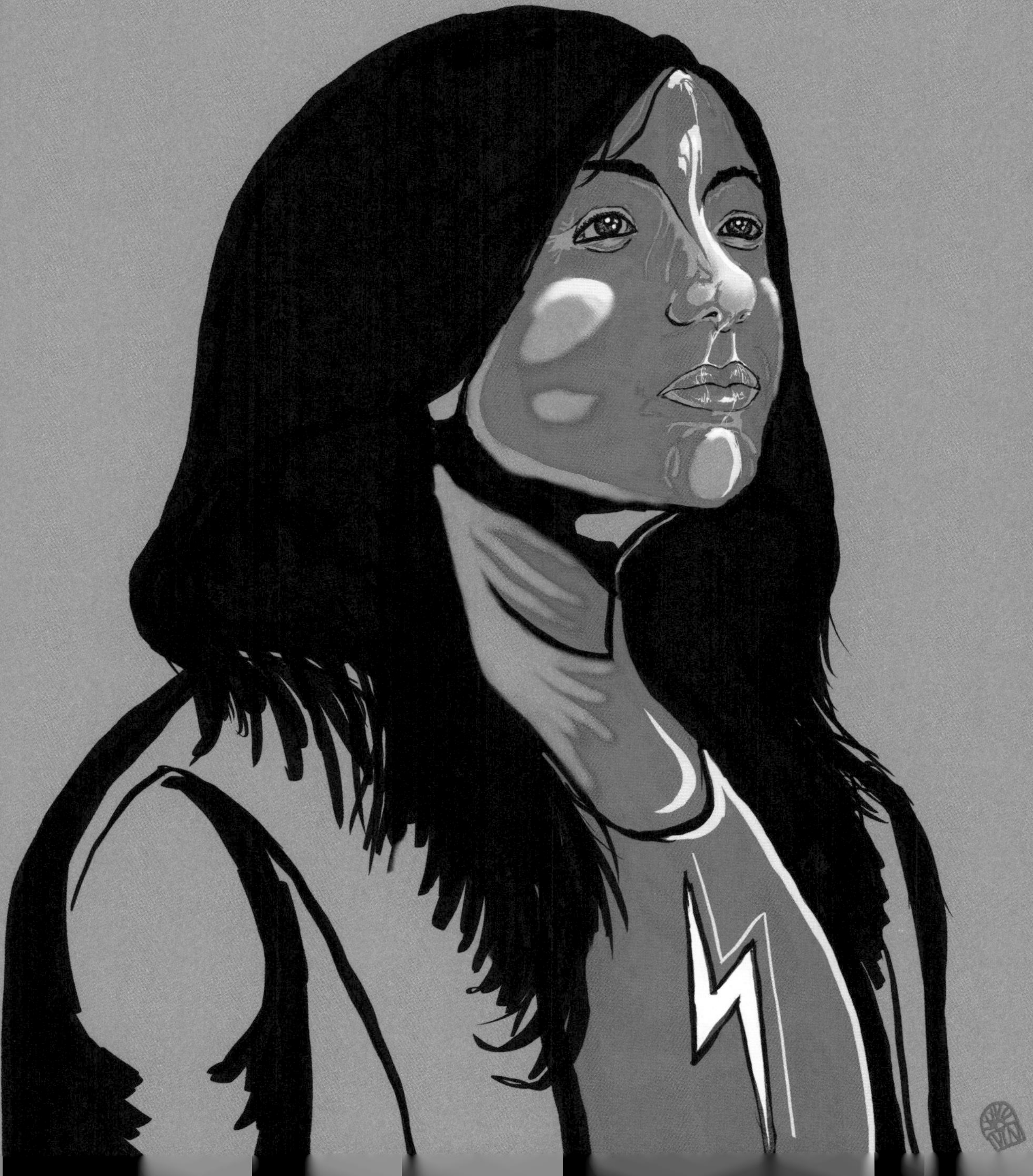

BEGUM SAMRU

INSTINCTIVE LEADER

'JEWEL AMONG WOMEN.'

This was the title bestowed on Begum Samru by the Mughal emperor of India for her bravery, beauty and loyalty when she rescued him after he'd been kidnapped by his enemies.

Born Farzana Zeb-un-Nissa, she fled to Delhi with her mother after her father's death. Misfortune struck again when Farzana's mother also died soon after. Orphaned and homeless, Farzana now had to make ends meet, so she began to work as a dancer. In 1767, her fortunes drastically changed when she met Walter Reinhardt. This soldier worked for the ruler of Bengal and was nicknamed General Sombre. It was love at first sight and they soon married. Farzana changed her name to Begum Samru, which was her interpretation of his nickname.

Begum Samru took a keen interest in her husband's work. The couple were charming leaders and the Mughal rulers liked them so much that they made Walter the ruler of the kingdom of Sardhana.

Begum Samru took control after her husband's death. Over a long and eventful reign, she became known for her remarkable negotiating skills and for fearlessly leading troops into battle. Begum Samru's survival instincts were legendary – she regained control of her kingdom after being imprisoned by mutineers, convinced Sikh invaders not to attack the Mughal emperor's territory, and even persuaded the British to leave Sardhana alone while they conquered neighbouring lands. People were so overwhelmed by her success they even started a rumour that she was using witchcraft to defeat her enemies.

Possessing extraordinary ability and charm, Begum Samru skilfully maintained power for over half a century up until her death.

BORN: ABOUT 1753   DIED: 27 JANUARY 1836 (AGED 82)
COUNTRY OF BIRTH: PRESENT-DAY INDIA

RACHEL ROY

INCLUSIVE FASHION DESIGNER

'WOMEN SHOULD WEAR CLOTHING; CLOTHING SHOULDN'T WEAR WOMEN.'

Rachel spotted a gap in the fashion market and saw an opportunity to help women feel confident about being both powerful and feminine in the workplace.

Rachel credits her success to her Indian father. He valued hard work and discipline and wanted his daughter to embrace these principles. At the age of fourteen, he dropped her off at the shopping mall and told her not to come home until she'd got a job. Rachel rose to the challenge and managed to secure a job in a clothing store.

After university, Rachel moved to New York to be at the heart of the global fashion industry. She worked as a wardrobe stylist and interned at Rocawear, a clothing company co-founded by rapper JAY-Z. Rachel's talent and drive saw her rise to the top, eventually becoming Rocawear's creative director of women and children's fashion.

Taking inspiration from old movies, in which women's clothes were both strong and feminine, Rachel went on to create her own clothing line company. Her designs helped businesswomen, regardless of body type, stand out from the crowd while still looking professional. Rachel's brand is now global and she has dressed some of the world's most famous women, including Michelle Obama, Oprah Winfrey and Kim Kardashian.

While expanding her business empire, Rachel founded Kindness Is Always Fashionable. This charity helps women across the world to earn a living income to support their families and communities. Rachel has also published a number of books and starred in television shows.

Rachel's unique creations have helped women and young girls of different shapes and sizes feel positive in the clothes they wear.

BORN: 15 JANUARY 1974

COUNTRY OF BIRTH: UNITED STATES OF AMERICA

ILLUSTRATION BY
KOKILA BHATTACHARYA

SUNAINA SETHI

SAVVY RESTAURATEUR

'JUST BE CONFIDENT.'

Sunaina whispers these three words to herself before opening the doors to her newest restaurant. A long line of excited customers have been waiting outside for hours. This is the scene at most of Sunaina's award-winning restaurants across London every night.

Sunaina was born and raised in London with her two brothers. As a child, she dreamed about many different careers, ranging from postwoman to astronaut. After university, she decided to try her hand at finance and moved to Germany to work for a bank.

Sunaina returned to London two years later and started helping out at her family's restaurant, Trishna, while she looked for a new job. After just three days, Sunaina abandoned her job search – she loved working at the restaurant and realized this was her true calling.

Eager to contribute to the business, she began training to become a sommelier – a wine expert. Sommeliers are traditionally males, so this journey wasn't easy for Sunaina – during one of her first training sessions, she was the only woman in a room filled with fifteen men!

Now a fully qualified sommelier, Sunaina is responsible for ensuring the guests in all her restaurants have a delightful culinary experience. Sunaina and her brothers have steadily grown their business empire and now own and run some of the best restaurants in the UK.

Confidence has been the secret ingredient in Sunaina's recipe for success. Sunaina gives some of that confidence to other aspiring restaurateurs by investing in their ideas and helping them get started.

BORN: 31 OCTOBER 1987

COUNTRY OF BIRTH: UNITED KINGDOM

YOUR STORY

YOUR NAME

_____

DESCRIBE YOURSELF

_____

WHAT'S YOUR STORY?

_____   _____
_____   _____
_____   _____
_____   _____
_____   _____
_____   _____
_____   _____
_____   _____
_____   _____
_____   _____
_____   _____
_____   _____
_____   _____
_____   _____
_____   _____
_____   _____
_____   _____

BORN: _____

COUNTRY OF BIRTH: _____

YOUR PORTRAIT

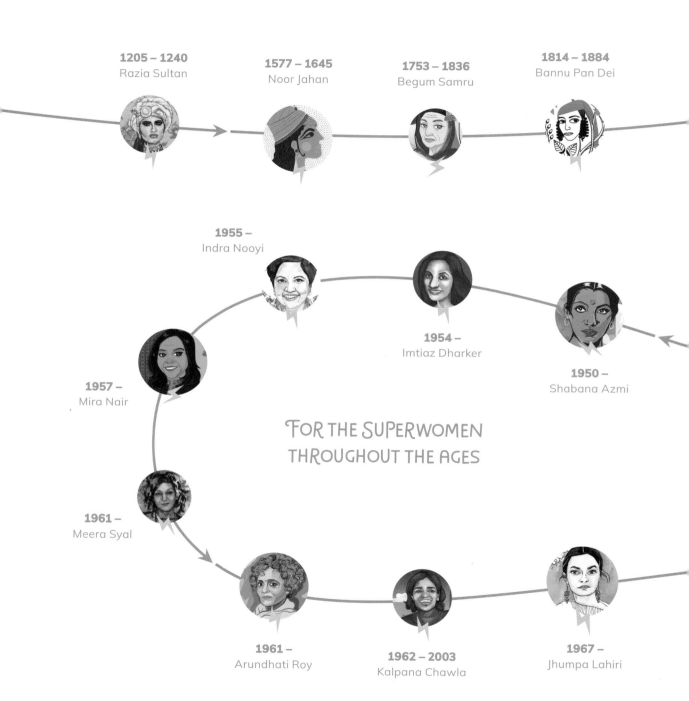

1205 – 1240
Razia Sultan

1577 – 1645
Noor Jahan

1753 – 1836
Begum Samru

1814 – 1884
Bannu Pan Dei

1955 –
Indra Nooyi

1954 –
Imtiaz Dharker

1950 –
Shabana Azmi

1957 –
Mira Nair

1961 –
Meera Syal

FOR THE SUPERWOMEN
THROUGHOUT THE AGES

1961 –
Arundhati Roy

1962 – 2003
Kalpana Chawla

1967 –
Jhumpa Lahiri

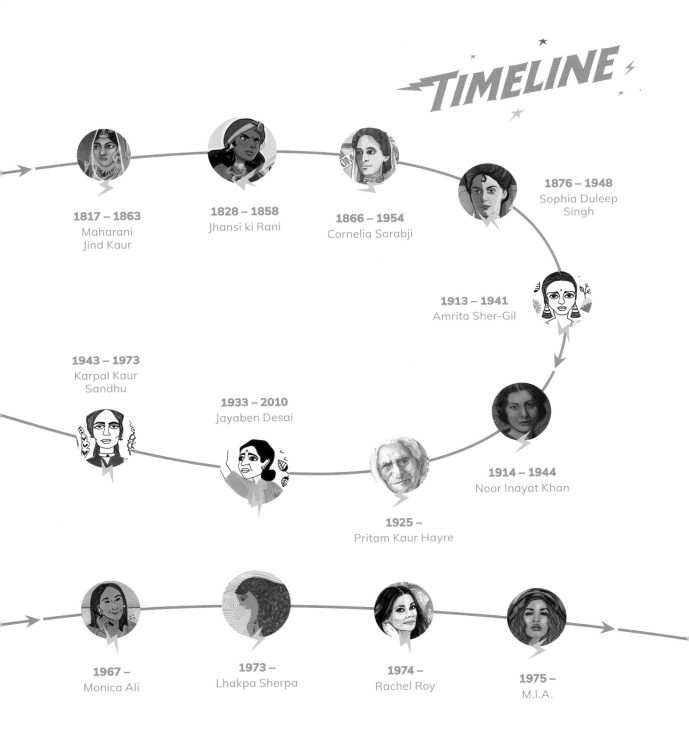

TIMELINE

1817 – 1863
Maharani
Jind Kaur

1828 – 1858
Jhansi ki Rani

1866 – 1954
Cornelia Sorabji

1876 – 1948
Sophia Duleep
Singh

1913 – 1941
Amrita Sher-Gil

1943 – 1973
Karpal Kaur
Sandhu

1933 – 2010
Jayaben Desai

1925 –
Pritam Kaur Hayre

1914 – 1944
Noor Inayat Khan

1967 –
Monica Ali

1973 –
Lhakpa Sherpa

1974 –
Rachel Roy

1975 –
M.I.A.

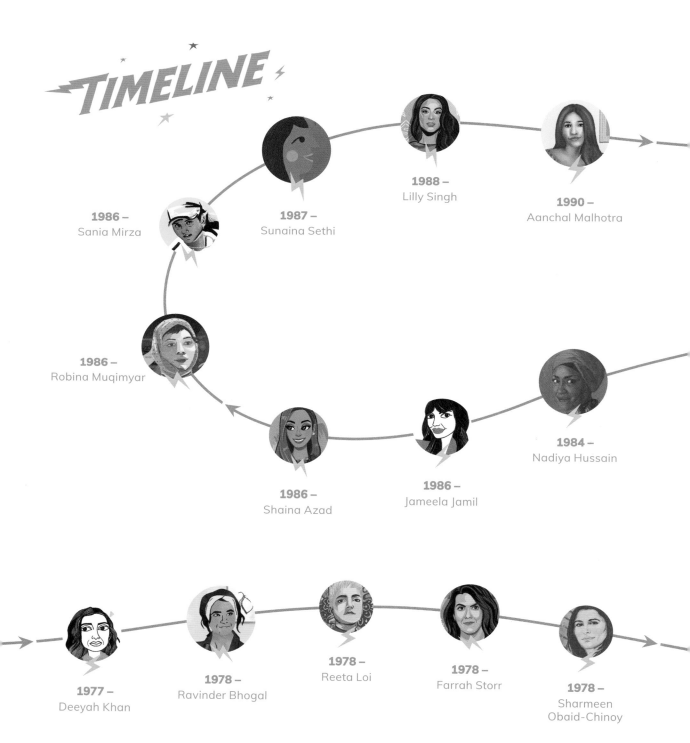

TIMELINE

1986 – Sania Mirza

1987 – Sunaina Sethi

1988 – Lilly Singh

1990 – Aanchal Malhotra

1986 – Robina Muqimyar

1986 – Shaina Azad

1986 – Jameela Jamil

1984 – Nadiya Hussain

1977 – Deeyah Khan

1978 – Ravinder Bhogal

1978 – Reeta Loi

1978 – Farrah Storr

1978 – Sharmeen Obaid-Chinoy

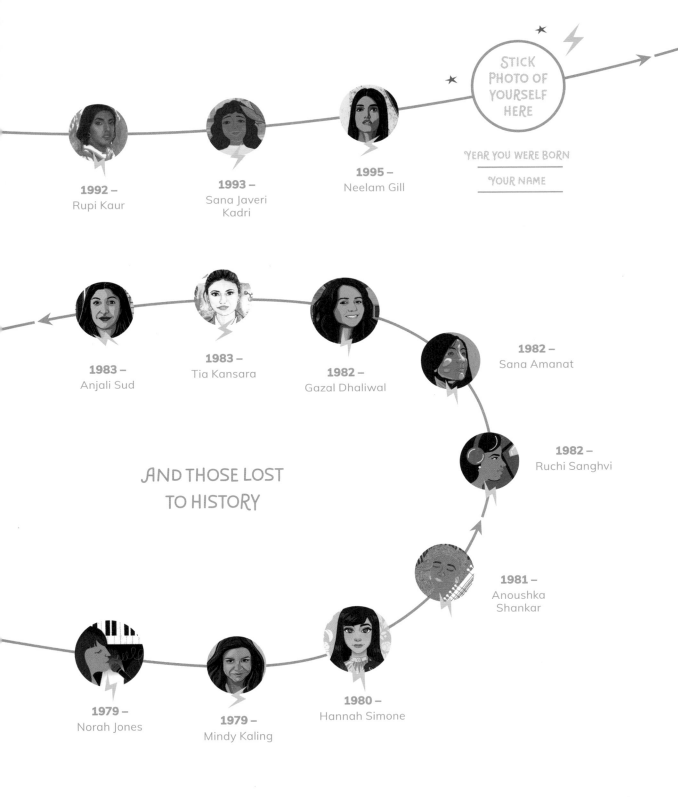

1992 –
Rupi Kaur

1993 –
Sana Javeri Kadri

1995 –
Neelam Gill

STICK PHOTO OF YOURSELF HERE

YEAR YOU WERE BORN

YOUR NAME

1983 –
Anjali Sud

1983 –
Tia Kansara

1982 –
Gazal Dhaliwal

1982 –
Sana Amanat

1982 –
Ruchi Sanghvi

AND THOSE LOST TO HISTORY

1981 –
Anoushka Shankar

1979 –
Norah Jones

1979 –
Mindy Kaling

1980 –
Hannah Simone

ANU CHOUHAN

BORN: 1988   COUNTRY OF BIRTH: CANADA

Introduce yourself.
I am an illustrator and animator who specializes in character design.

Who is your favourite superwoman?
Rani Lakhshmi Bai (Jhansi ki Rani) and Mai Bhago.

How have they inspired you?
I love that they were warriors and leaders, during a time when women were not normally allowed on the battlefield. They were both courageous and confident, and stood up for what was important to them.

How did you get into the world of art?
As a child, I used to doodle while watching cartoons. I also discovered video games at a very young age, which helped spark my imagination and got me interested in character design. After high school I studied graphic design and animation, and soon after began working as a mobile game artist. That was when I started posting my artwork as Anumation on social media as well!

Who are your favourite artists?
Two illustrators that I have admired for a long time and that I often think of are Katsuya Terada and Ai Yazawa. Terada's art is surreal and dreamy, and he created artwork for some of my favourite video games growing up. Yazawa is a famous manga artist, I love the way she illustrates her expressive characters. It's also thanks to her art that I got into fashion!

If you could be remembered for one thing, what would it be?
My art, namely the stories that I was able to tell through my work.

What's the biggest lesson in life you've learned so far?
Even if you work really hard, that does not automatically mean success is guaranteed. The important thing is to stay motivated and learn from your mistakes along the way.

What advice would you give to young South Asian Supergirls growing up?
Live your life for yourself. If you are passionate about something, go and pursue it and don't let others make you doubt yourself or your potential.

ILLUSTRATIONS:
PAGES 28, 62, 74, 84 & 96

DEEPIKAH R. BHARDWAJ

BORN: 1985   COUNTRY OF BIRTH: INDIA

Introduce yourself.
I am a multidisciplinary artist based in Bangalore, India. I use digital illustration and installation art to express issues related to gender, society, self-worth

Who is your favourite superwoman?
Kalpana Chawla has been my favourite superwoman since I read about her as a child.

How has she inspired you?
She came from a very humble background. But that didn't stop her from being so outstanding in everything she did. I got curious about the universe because of her and that has helped me in many ways and inspired some of my work.

How did you get into the world of art?
I worked as a designer and illustrator for a while. But only the field of art is fluid and without boundaries, which allowed me to express everything that I wanted to.

Who is your favourite artist?
Seema Kohli is one of my favourite artists. Her work is extremely layered and colourful – you can make up your own stories from just looking at it. On a personal note, because she is a mother and an artist, it gives me a lot of hope and courage about what women can achieve – that being a mother is a strength and not a limitation.

If you could be remembered for one thing, what would it be?
I would like to be remembered for pointing fingers, shouting loudly and making a fuss about all the wrongs in Indian society.

What's the biggest lesson in life you've learned so far?
'Aham Brahmasmi' or 'I am God'. Roughly translated, it means I am not separate from my Creator. I have and I am everything I need or want.

What advice would you give to young South Asian Supergirls growing up?
Do not stay quiet. Listen to your thoughts and inner voice, they are important.

Instagram: @deepikah   Twitter: @deepikah   Facebook: DeepikahCo   www.deepikah.co

ILLUSTRATIONS:
PAGES 14, 38, 42, 54 & 80

KOKILA BHATTACHARYA

BORN: 1993   COUNTRY OF BIRTH: INDIA

Introduce yourself.
I'm a freelance illustrator, social activist and accidental entrepreneur with a penchant for dreams and slumber.

Who is your favourite superwoman?
Soni Sori and the thousands of Adivasi women in India. Soni Sori is a teacher turned firebrand activist from Bastar in the war-torn state of Chhattisgarh, India. Despite enduring torture and abuse from the state authorities, police and other forces, she continues to fight atrocities committed against the Adivasis (tribals) and indigenous communities.

How have they inspired you?
Every time I find myself in a difficult situation, their story and struggle is a reminder of two things: it could be much worse, and you can still fight it.

How did you get into the world of art?
I was told by my parents that I started to scribble before I started speaking. So I believe I entered the world of art by being born.

Who is your favourite artist?
Hayao Miyazaki's animation stirs my love for storytelling and leaves me with a sense of compassion. Grant Snider's comics rekindle the curiosity, and artists like Thenmozhi Soundararajan (Dalits-rights activist) and Malik Sajad (graphic novelist based in Kashmir) help drive personal expression for socio-political change.

If you could be remembered for one thing, what would it be?
Creating a forest. With depleting world resources, we need to recreate self-sustaining ecosystems.

What's the biggest lesson in life you've learned so far?
Being alive is a privilege that must be used for something greater than life.

What advice would you give to young South Asian Supergirls growing up?
Question everything you feel bound by. Do not give in to societal pressure and definitions. Support each other's voices.

Instagram: @kokilab   Twitter: @KokilaB   Facebook: kokila.nirvana

MEENAL PATEL

BORN: 1984   COUNTRY OF BIRTH: UNITED STATES OF AMERICA

Introduce yourself.
I am an artist, illustrator and children's book author.

Who is your favourite superwoman?
My mom, Gita.

How has she inspired you?
She has shown me that it's possible to be strong and gentle, quiet and commanding, all at the same time. She has shown me that strength manifests in different forms for different people.

How did you get into the world of art?
I have learned that I can express my ideas best through visual art or writing rather than spoken words. I also love the act of making something out of nothing, especially when what I make connects with another person. The magic is in that connection.

Who is your favourite artist?
One of my favourite artists is Sanna Annukka. I love how she creates visual stories in her art that weave in her family's heritage. She does it in a way that makes her pieces feel like historic artefacts and at the same time so modern.

If you could be remembered for one thing, what would it be?
Fiercely caring for others, whether I know them or not.

What's the biggest lesson in life you've learned so far?
Everyone is going through something difficult even if you cannot see it on the outside.

What advice would you give to young South Asian Supergirls growing up?
All of your identities matter and are valuable pieces of your story. Those pieces make you multidimensional and are worthy of sharing with others.

Instagram: @meenal_land   Facebook: meenalpatelstudio   www.meenalpatelstudio.com

ILLUSTRATIONS:
PAGES 2, 16, 26, 50, 86 & 100

Nazrina Rodjan

BORN: 1990   COUNTRY OF BIRTH: THE NETHERLANDS

Introduce yourself.
I am an artist who wants all children to be able to see themselves in stories.

Who is your favourite superwomen?
My favourite superwomen are my two older sisters, Sabrina and Farina.

How have they inspired you?
I know they will always be there for me, no matter what. They taught me how to love unconditionally and I would never be where I am today without their support.

How did you get into the world of art?
What inspired me to pursue art as a career were the comics and picture books I read as a kid. I loved to create new worlds by drawing and I knew I wanted to go to art school from the age of eight.

Who is your favourite artist?
Shaun Tan is my favourite artist because he can tell beautiful stories and creates emotion in picture books without using any words. His stunning artworks are enough.

If you could be remembered for one thing, what would it be?
I would want to be remembered for creating stories and artworks that inspire the next generations to make their voices heard.

What's the biggest lesson in life you've learned so far?
Nothing ever goes smoothly or according to plan, but by keeping my eyes on my goal, which was to make a career out of something I love, I was able to achieve my dream of becoming an artist.

What advice would you give to young South Asian Supergirls growing up?
Find out what you really want, so you can go after it full force. Don't be scared to fail, it's just a learning experience. And don't worry too much about pleasing others. Sometimes you have to disrupt things to stay true to yourself.

Instagram: @hiddenlionstudio   Facebook: hiddenlionstudio   www.hiddenlionstudio.com

ILLUSTRATIONS:
PAGES 4, 34, 58 & 90

POONAM SAINI

BORN: 1992   COUNTRY OF BIRTH: UNITED KINGDOM

Introduce yourself.
Formally, I'm co-founder and director of Kiss Branding, a brand design studio in Leeds. Informally, I'm a big earring-wearing, sausage dog fanatic who makes silly noises and sings loudly when I work.

Who is your favourite superwoman?
My mum, Surinder.

How has she inspired you?
Surinder is an exceptionally talented chef and tailor. She came from India with fantastic talents and skills but no one helped her leverage them into opportunities. I found this totally unfair. This lack of appreciation and recognition fired my soul to set up my own business and help people who should be valued and celebrated.

How did you get into the world of art?
Art was always my strength at school; however, culturally, it's not seen as a worthwhile career. So I wanted to prove everyone wrong. I studied hard, worked with some of the best creative people in London and then set up my own design studio.

Who is your favourite artist?
René Gruau. He captures the strength and confidence of women in just a few brush strokes.

If you could be remembered for one thing, what would it be?
Making people feel better about themselves and being an honest, loving friend.

What's the biggest lesson in life you've learned so far?
Adults are not always right, sometimes they make mistakes and feel lost just as much as children, and that's okay. Don't forget, young people can inspire and teach just as much as older people.

What advice would you give to young South Asian Supergirls growing up?
Challenge the way things are done in the world through reading, learning and listening to others. Don't stay quiet, keep an open mind and stand up for good people and their ideas. Look after your mental well-being, have plenty of sleep every day and work together as supergirls with boys to make a better world for us all!

Instagram: @in_saini / @kiss_branding   www.kissbranding.co.uk

RAJVINDER KAUR

BORN: 1978   COUNTRY OF BIRTH: UNITED KINGDOM

Introduce yourself.
I am a graphic designer, artist and illustrator.

Who is your favourite superwoman?
My grandmother! She was a strong-spirited, fiery woman who had a strong presence in the room. She welcomed everyone into our home, filling it with laughter and food.

How has she inspired you?
She had the spirit of a fearless warrior with a huge open heart. When I feel the need for inner strength, I always think of her and how she went through so many life challenges, and still came through fighting strong.

How did you get into the world of art?
I have always sketched and painted ever since I was a child, loving the feeling and escapism of making pictures. Studying art and design was a natural step to take, but I wasn't sure how to make it a 'job'. I fell in love with graphic design, because I wanted to make everyday commercial art that everyone could experience, so I studied at Central St Martins in London. A few years later, I picked up my personal artwork in my own time, and soon I was exhibiting too!

Who is your favourite artist?
I have so many! If I had to pick one, it would be Amrita Sher-Gil. I'm fascinated with everything about her – her exotic, mysterious life, the fact that she challenged so many social norms and expectations of her, and of course her incredible artworks.

If you could be remembered for one thing, what would it be?
That I was never scared to do anything. I love Yoda's mantra that there is no try, there is only do or do not. That always pushes me into action!

What's the biggest lesson in life you've learned so far?
You never know what is around the corner, but that's okay. Smile and have fun anyway.

What advice would you give to young South Asian Supergirls growing up?
Never feel alone, and never doubt your value in this world. Live on your own terms. Always be kind, to yourself especially! Finally, the sisterhood is always there to support you, hold you and love you!

Instagram: @rajkaurartist   Twitter: @rajkaurcreates   Facebook: Raj Kaur Art   www.rajkaurart.com

Raj Kaur.

SANDEEP JOHAL

BORN: 1975   COUNTRY OF BIRTH: CANADA

Introduce yourself.
I am a visual artist who draws, paints and creates large-scale murals. I believe in the power of art to empower and effect meaningful change.

Who is your favourite superwoman?
I can't think of one specifically, but I'm grateful to all of the female trailblazers who have come before me and to all of the women now working hard to ensure equality and justice for women.

How did you get into the world of art?
I have been drawing obsessively since I was a child, went to art school at thirty, and became a professional artist at forty after becoming a mother in 2015.

Who is your favourite artist?
There are so many, but one that always comes to mind is Pakistani-raised contemporary artist Sara Khan. She is a highly skilled watercolourist who creates detailed, multilayered scenes that show the humour, beauty and ugliness of everyday life.

If you could be remembered for one thing, what would it be?
That my art made a positive impact and helped create a better world, especially for women.

What's the biggest lesson in life you've learned so far?
Anything worth doing takes time. Stay focused, work hard and trust yourself.

What advice would you give to young South Asian Supergirls growing up?
Believe in yourself. If you believe in yourself, anything is possible.

Instagram: @sandeepjohalart   Facebook: sandeepjohalART   www.sandeepjohal.com

ILLUSTRATIONS:
PAGES 6, 18, 36, 60, 68 & 82

SUMAN KAUR

BORN: 1987   COUNTRY OF BIRTH: UNITED KINGDOM

Introduce yourself.
I'm a fine artist with an interest in portraiture.

Who is your favourite superwoman?
My nan. Famous for being my grandma. She sees herself as the main beacon for the family.

How has she inspired you?
My nan is my muse. She's a vibrant, large personality who never fails to inspire me or my work. She's quite a stubborn person and does things her way, she interrupts, sings too loud in public, falls asleep a lot and wears mismatched bright clothes, which visually is interesting.

How did you get into the world of art?
In Year 5, when asked what I wanted to be when I grew up, I replied 'an artist'. I drew from an early age with enthusiasm for observational drawing and loved art. Years later, after doing a job in healthcare, I left to pursue my dream of being a full-time artist. Later that same year, I went on to win a national art competition on BBC1 called the *The Big Painting Challenge*. I guess that was my first real step to focusing on art professionally.

Who is your favourite artist?
That's really hard to answer. I love anything with soul that is alive with energy. I love to see skill in the work and emotions of the reality of life – so maybe Degas, Francis Bacon or Da Vinci because he was a polymath. John Singer Sargent is amazing too. I can't decide! It changes!

If you could be remembered for one thing, what would it be?
Being an important artist in history.

What's the biggest lesson in life you've learned so far?
The path to success is not always the easiest.

What advice would you give to young South Asian Supergirls growing up?
Never listen to people who say you can't achieve your goals.

Instagram: @87skart   Twitter: @sumankaurart   Facebook: skart87

VINNY SOOR

BORN: 1977   COUNTRY OF BIRTH: TANZANIA

Introduce yourself.

I'm an artist and development consultant, creating humanity- and wildlife-inspired artwork, usually charged with emotion.

Who is your favourite superwoman?

I've too many across generations, continents, cultures and genres! Here's a few: Kali Maa, Durga Mata, Bebe Nanaki, Mata Gujri, Noor Jahan, Lata Mangeshkar, Coretta Scott King, Maya Angelou, Oprah Winfrey, Iyanla Vanzant, Arundhati Roy, my nani-ji and dhadhi-ji.

How have they inspired you?

They've all taught me the importance of perseverance (if you want to achieve something, keep working towards it), strength (it comes in all shapes and sizes), love and positivity (never be afraid to challenge wrongs and stereotypes around you).

How did you get into the world of art?

I was five years old when my Australian teacher picked up a flower drawing of mine and said it was the most amazing and accurate thing she had ever seen from someone my age. That feeling never left me. I'm continually inspired by the colours of my heritage and homelands.

Who is your favourite artist?

Again I have lots! A sprinkling would be: Da Vinci for his curiosity, Klimt for his daring, Tagore for his thought, Dalí for his madness, Banerjee for her colour and Kusama for her eccentricity.

If you could be remembered for one thing, what would it be?

Being both tough and kind, and knowing when to choose either.

What's the biggest lesson in life you've learned so far?

Nothing is forever, let go with gladness, enjoy what you love, laugh often, and forgiveness in its own time is a miracle.

What advice would you give to young South Asian Supergirls growing up?

You are unique and can do anything you put your mind to! Dream big and remember mistakes are just opportunities to learn. Never, ever (not in a gazillion years) give up!

Instagram: @vinnysoorcreates   Facebook: VinnyHasVaVaVoom   www.vinnysworld.co.uk

ILLUSTRATIONS:
PAGES 20, 70, 88 & 94

ACKNOWLEDGEMENTS

This book is dedicated to my grandmothers who were the superwomen in my life.

Highest thanks and gratitude to the Almighty Waheguru without whom nothing is possible.

I'd like to also thank my family, friends and colleagues for their support, in particular: my parents, Susan and Onkar, for their relentless support; my siblings, Jaupreet and Jujhar, for being born and setting the Pink Ladoo Project in motion; Adam – for patiently entertaining my excitement and despair (which came in equal measure) throughout this book's journey; Sonny, for being my guinea pig (and for saying 'and she didn't even know it?' when I told you Rupi Kaur is a poet); Abi Fellows, for being the best agent ever; Rachel Hard and Andrea MacDonald for being wonderful editors and making my dreams come true by bringing this project to Penguin; Matt & Poonam (the dynamic design duo behind Kiss Branding) for turning my thoughts into ideas and those ideas into art; and Mona Kalantar for helping me literally sketch out my vision for this book all those years ago and encouraging me to make that vision a reality.

Thank you to each of the ten artists who contributed amazing artwork to this project and brought it to life.

Thank you to Lois Stamps and Blaize Blackmon for doing late-in-the-day editing on the very first edition of this book (and in Blaize's case, while also waiting to be induced for labour!).

Thanks also to Amrit Kaur Jodha, Simran Kaur Jodha, Sukhdeep Singh, Jup Kaur, Keerit Kaur, Saroop Kaur, Rita Dhaliwal, Alpie Patel, Salma Ishaque, Kina Chana, Gurpal Virdi, the Police Review, the sales team at Allison & Busby and FMcM Associates.

Finally, I'd like to extend an enormous thanks to Parmjit Singh, Dr Bik and everyone else who makes up the Kashi House team. None of this would have happened if Kashi House hadn't risked their time, money and reputation on me and published the very first edition of this book in 2019. They are a gem and prove why independent publishers are more crucial than ever. My royalties from this book will continue to go to charity, with a portion also being donated to Kashi House CIC so they can continue to fund ground-breaking literary projects.

ABOUT THE AUTHOR

RAJ KAUR KHAIRA

RAJ KAUR KHAIRA's lifelong passion for gender equality led her to founding the Pink Ladoo Project in 2015. This innovative initiative, which encourages the equal treatment of newborn girls in South Asian families, has attracted tens of thousands of followers in communities across the UK, Canada, the US and Australia. It has rapidly become one of the most prominent feminist movements for South Asian women globally, and propelled Raj to becoming an influential and credible thought leader.

Raj lives in London.

Raj will be donating 100% of author proceeds from the sales of this book to charities supporting women and children.

★ www.pinkladoo.org
★ Instagram: @pinkladoo
★ Facebook: pinkladoo